5-INGREDIENT ONE-POT COOKBOOK

5-INGREDIENT
one-pot
COOKBOOK

EASY DINNERS FROM YOUR SKILLET, DUTCH OVEN, SHEET PAN & MORE

Linda Kurniadi

PHOTOGRAPHY BY NADINE GREEFF

**ROCKRIDGE
PRESS**

Designer: Kristine Brogno
Editor: Vanessa Ta
Production Editor: Erum Khan
Photography: © 2018 Nadine Greeff

ISBN: Print 978-1-64152-141-3 | eBook 978-1-64152-142-0

To my husband, Frederick Kurniadi,
and my family, for your endless support.
To dark chocolate, my companion
through many a long night of writing.
To you (yes, you)!

Contents

7 Roasting Pan

8 No-Cook Bowl

Introduction

HAVE YOU EVER WISHED you had a magical kitchen where you could prepare delicious and healthy food? Perhaps you work in an office with a busy schedule and tight deadlines. Or maybe you are a stay-at-home parent looking after your family. We live in a busy, fast-paced world where everything needs to be done quickly and time is a limited commodity. To all you busy people out there—I feel you.

When I first started my blog, SimplyHealthyish.com, I had no idea where it would lead. At the time, my only goal was to share my favorite recipes with others who love food, too. But my life has changed a lot since then. I started working up to 100 hours a week in a corporate office. I dreamed of the day I could walk into my home after a long day and have dinner whipped up in minutes.

I can't tell you how many times I wished I could stay at home wearing my stretchy pants and creating wholesome homemade meals that my hubby and I could enjoy together. I know it sounds like wishful thinking, but I decided to make it a reality by picking up my pots and pans to make some comfort food. After all the chaos I went through at the office, cooking became the highlight of my day, the thing I enjoyed most. So I was always looking forward to creating fresh, quick, delicious, and comforting meals to make after a hard day at work.

Although I am incredibly grateful for everything I have in my life, one dream always stayed the same: to cook and share my cooking with family, friends, and all of you. And here we are.

Cooking is not a genetically inherited skill. Just because your mom or grandmother is a good cook doesn't mean you will be, too. Cooking is something you need to spend time doing to improve—just like all skills in life. I'm a self-taught cook and love quick, easy recipes that put a smile on my face.

The recipes I set out to make are simple, so if you are busy with work or kids, or you are new to cooking, my recipes will help you move past any fears you may have and will increase the fun factor as you explore different flavors. Once you become a bit more adventurous, you can tweak the recipes to suit your tastes. If you lead a busy lifestyle, this book will work like magic for you, too.

Every recipe in this book is made with five ingredients or less (not counting oil, salt, pepper, water, and nonstick cooking spray) and in one pot or pan. Most of the recipes can be on the table in 30 minutes or less, and some of them can be made in a slow cooker. Many can be prepared when you have some time and frozen for quick reheating later.

My goal with this book is to show you how easy it is to make a delicious dinner without spending hours in the kitchen. Most importantly, my biggest focus is to use fresh ingredients as much as possible and keep processed foods to a minimum.

I believe we can all eat healthy, fresh meals if we know where to start. Here you'll find a celebration of variety, color, and balance. The dinner struggle ends today!

Easy One-Pot Cooking

I have always loved creating quick and simple recipes that are delicious and packed full of flavor. And after a busy day at work and being stuck in traffic, there is nothing more satisfying than a hearty, delicious, home-cooked meal.

No one should have to choose between eating healthy and making quick meals. So I'm glad you are here to discover one-pot, five-ingredient recipes that are made with fresh, flavorful ingredients. These recipes will make your life simpler, especially when you don't feel like cooking.

Truly Easy

This book is perfect when you need a meal that is satisfying and tasty and doesn't take hours to make but still focuses on fresh ingredients and bold flavors. Every recipe you will find here is made with five ingredients or less (not counting a few basics) and in just one pot or pan. Plus, you can get all the ingredients needed for the recipes here from one grocery store or farmers' market, rather than visiting a few specialty stores to hunt down the items.

This book emphasizes simplicity in cooking. While creating the recipes, I surprised even myself with how delicious these quick dishes are. Cooking with fewer ingredients can be very liberating, as you really taste the flavor of each individual ingredient. Nothing is overpowered, and less is definitely more.

Would you believe me if I told you that you can make simple, healthyish chicken cordon bleu with just five ingredients? You definitely can, if you focus on the key ingredient combinations that enable you to maximize the flavors in the dish.

I include vegetables in my dishes whenever possible, which helps streamline dinnertime. Adding veggies to dishes gives you a larger portion size with a fraction of the calories. Plus you'll get more of those healthy nutrients.

A short list of ingredients also means these recipes are simple and quick to prepare. And, you don't have to worry about being overwhelmed, because all of them are easy to master, even for beginner cooks. You can create a pot or pan of sumptuous comfort food in just minutes, without the mess or fuss of traditional cooking,

while still packing in all the familiar flavors of Mom's (or Dad's) home cooking.

One-Pot Wonderful

When you are faced with the challenge of making a meal from scratch and then cleaning up versus a convenient yet unhealthy takeout meal, the simplest process normally wins. We have all been there.

Preparation, therefore, needs to be quick and easy, but it's just as important to think about cleanup. At the end of your workday, cleaning is the last thing you feel like doing, so making things as simple as possible is the key to staying away from the takeout. This is a one-pot cookbook, so cleanup is limited to just one pot and maybe a few prep items.

This book focuses on primarily using fresh ingredients and keeps processed foods to a minimum. In a world where sugar and salt are added in excess to most foods, you can keep track of what you are eating when you're cooking for yourself and your family. This goes a long way toward helping you live a healthier life. Plus, when you start cooking using fresh ingredients, you will realize how much better they taste.

Many of the recipes here use fresh ingredients, but you can easily use frozen, as well. For example, if you'd like to make a recipe calling for Brussels sprouts (which are typically an autumn and winter vegetable) in summer, consider using frozen Brussels sprouts instead. Or you can mix and match other seasonal vegetables as you like.

While it may sound difficult to make homemade food that is healthy and tasty, you will soon see that you can create beautiful meals in the same amount of time it takes to wait for takeout. You will also save money cooking at home. One-pot cooking is an easy, stress-free way to prepare fast, healthy dinners.

One Pot, One Pan . . .

One pot does not mean one way of cooking or one type of food. In this book, you will find 120 recipes that are perfect for everything from busy weeknight dinners to play dates to dinner parties. You will find easy ways to make all of your favorite foods. Many of these dishes are my interpretation of comfort foods that I truly enjoy and that are easy to make with whole-some ingredients.

In fact, there's so much variety that when you scan the recipe lists, you may have a hard time figuring out what to make first and even wonder where on earth to start. Don't worry; I'm here for you. Are you having a fancy din-ner party or date night tonight? Try the Steak Seared in Browned Butter (page 77). Do you have a craving for something warm and whole-some? Spicy Sausage and Kale Soup (page 65) is your answer. Don't feel like cooking tonight and want something extra quick? Whip up the Chicken Satay Zoodles Bowl (page 142).

When it comes to the tools you need to make the recipes, you don't need a profession-ally equipped kitchen. Most of these dishes can be made using small or medium pots and pans, which work perfectly for a family of two to four people. In fact, you probably have almost everything you need in your kitchen cabinets right now.

Here's a little introduction to each of the pots and pans you'll be using to cook the recipes in this book. In each chapter, you will find even more information and tips on each specific cooking vessel. Bear in mind that if you're buying new cookware, a set of pots and pans is often a better deal than getting individual pieces. Always buy the highest-quality tools that your budget will allow, too, because they will last longer than lower-quality cookware.

Skillet

A skillet, also known as a frying pan, is ideal for frying, browning, and sautéing chicken, meat, eggs, fish, vegetables, and potatoes. It has low sides that flare out, making it easier to flip your food. Skillets range in size from around 6 inches up to 14 inches in diameter. In this book, I'll use an 8-inch and a 10-inch skillet, but you can choose one size and use it for everything. Learn more about skillets on page 15.

Sauté Pan

The difference between a skillet and a sauté pan is the shape. A sauté pan has straight sides and typically comes with a lid. In addition to doing all the things your skillet can do, it's also good for making thick sauces (like marinara) and searing. Sauté pans range in size from 10 to 14 inches across. For the recipes in this book, I use a 12-inch sauté pan. Learn more about sauté pans on page 15.

Saucepan

Whether you are cooking hard-boiled eggs or warming up last night's leftovers, a saucepan is your pot of choice. Saucepans range in size from around 2 cups to 4 quarts. Most have straight sides and are a moderate depth. All should come with a cover that fits tightly inside the rim. The recipes in this book use a 2-quart saucepan. Learn more about saucepans on page 37.

Stockpot

Stockpots are used to make broth or stock, which often serves as the base of recipes, and can also be used to boil pasta or steam vegetables. They have tall sides and a tight-fitting cover. In this book, I use a 5.5-quart stockpot. Learn more about stockpots on page 37.

Dutch Oven

A Dutch oven is a heavy pot that has a tight-fitting lid. It's safe to use on a stove top and in the oven, and it is the vessel of choice to slow cook braises and stews. They range in size from around 2 quarts to 8 quarts. For my recipes, I use a 5.5-quart size. If you don't have a Dutch oven, you can use a deep, ovenproof sauté pan—either with an ovenproof lid or covered with a piece of aluminum foil. Learn more about Dutch ovens on page 61.

Sheet Pan

A sheet pan is also called a baking sheet or a baking tray. It's a rectangular metal pan with a low rim that you put in the oven. It's most commonly used to bake pastries, bread rolls, and flat foods, like Swiss rolls (also known as jelly rolls), sheet cakes, cookies, and pizzas. But I also use my sheet pan to cook things like pork chops, salmon, and chicken. You will be fine with a half sheet pan, which is 18 by 13 inches, for the recipes here. Learn more about sheet pans on page 79.

Baking Dish

A baking dish is also called a casserole dish. It is a deep dish that can be put in the oven and used for things like braises, casseroles, and baked pasta dishes. The recipes in this book use a 4-quart rectangular baking dish (typically 14 by 10 by 2 inches). Learn more about baking dishes on page 103.

Roasting Pan

A roasting pan is most often used to oven roast poultry, meat, and vegetables and potatoes. It can be used with or without a rack that sits in the pan. This rack lifts the food above the juice and fat drippings and lets the air circulate all around the food. The ideal roasting plan should have sides that are 2 to 3 inches high, which ensures that the meat and juices are contained in the pan, while the heat can easily circulate. This means your meat will brown and crisp perfectly. Some roasting pans have straight sides, while others have sides that flare out, and both work equally well. It's great to have at least two roasting pans: a small, 9-by-13-inch pan and a medium, 10-by-14-inch pan. Learn more about roasting pans on page 121.

Bowl

You know what a bowl is! This round, deep vessel is used for mixing ingredients. The recipes in chapter 8 require no cooking, and many are simply mixed in a bowl. Learn more about mixing bowls on page 139.

COOKWARE

Each recipe in this book includes an icon to let you know which cooking vessel is used to prepare the dish.

ICON	VESSEL	SIZE	COOKING TECHNIQUES	TYPICAL DISHES
	Skillet	8-inch	Panfry, sauté, braise	Omelets, frittatas, vegetables
	Skillet	10-inch	Panfry, stir-fry, sauté, braise	Rice, noodles, stir-fries, pancakes
	Sauté pan, covered	3-quart	Braise, sauté, sear, simmer, stir-fry	Marinara sauce, rice, stir-fries
	Saucepan	2-quart	Boil, simmer	Soup, sauce, stew, rice, grains
	Stockpot, covered	5.5-quart	Boil, simmer, steam	Broth, soup, stew, pasta
	Dutch oven, covered	5.5-quart	Brown, braise, sauté, roast, slow cook, deep-fry	Meat, soup, pasta, stew, sauce
	Sheet pan	18-by-13-inch (half sheet)	Bake	Oven-baked chicken and fish, vegetables, pastries, bread, pizza, cookies
	Baking dish	4-quart (9-by-13-inch)	Roast, bake	Casseroles, stew, baked pasta
	Roasting pan	9-by-13-inch	Roast	Roasted meat, poultry, vegetables, potatoes, casseroles
	Roasting pan	10-by-14 inch	Roast	Roasted meat, poultry, vegetables, potatoes, lasagna

One-Pot Cooking with Slow Cookers and Pressure Cookers

For more than 30 years, the humble slow cooker has been many a home cook's favorite way to make one-pot meals. Today, the slow cooker is still a favorite, especially in the fall and winter. But slow cooking also has its limitations—such as *slow* cooking (it's in the name!), which means you need to plan and prep way in advance. Plus you're limited to things like soups and stews, and the results can sometimes be uneven.

Slow cookers also have many pros, including convenience, energy efficiency, safety, and the tenderness and flavor they bring even to inexpensive cuts of meat and other foods. Plus, they can save you time if you use them correctly.

Although slow cookers and pressure cookers are not the main cooking vessels for the recipes in this book, there are several recipes that can be made using your slow cooker, such as Sweet Potato Thai Curry Soup (page 48) and Sloppy Joe Sandwiches (page 74). For recipes that can be adapted to be made in a slow cooker, you'll find specific instructions in a "Cook It Slow" tip.

The Five-Ingredient Kitchen

While it is true that a well-planned shopping list is essential for a quick and efficient grocery store visit, if you stock your pantry with some basics, you won't have to go to the grocery store so often. You don't need to fill it up with exotic ingredients that you'll hardly ever use. Instead, give your pantry a makeover: Throw away all the old stuff that you can't even remember buying, and stock it with the things you'll need all the time.

The Basics

These items are the essentials for cooking most meals. They add zing and flavor, and they can also be used to make sauces and dressings. You'll use these ingredients in most of your dishes.

Olive oil: Although it is a bit expensive, buy genuine extra-virgin olive oil. It is great for lower-heat cooking, salads, and drizzling over dishes for a flourish. This is the only kind of oil I use in this book.

Nonstick cooking spray: I use a vegetable oil spray; it is much more efficient than greasing a pan and uses much less oil overall.

Salt: Salt brightens the taste of your food by bringing out the flavors. I keep fine-grain sea salt in my pantry. Table salt is more heavily processed to eliminate minerals and usually contains an additive to prevent clumping.

Black pepper: Freshly ground black pepper is great for breathing life into vegetables and meat.

Balsamic vinegar: This can be used in salad dressings, marinades, soups, and more. Balsamic vinegar is unparalleled in flavor—rich, tangy, and zesty—making it perfect for marinades and dressings. While there are all kinds of vinegars that add many wonderful flavors to foods, balsamic is the one I use in this book.

Pantry Staples

These are canned, boxed, and jarred ingredients that form the basis for many dishes.

Canned tuna: Find canned tuna that is low in mercury, sustainably sourced, and wild caught. I typically choose light tuna because the larger fish that are labeled white tuna have much higher mercury levels. And I prefer water-packed to oil-packed tuna because it has fewer calories and retains more healthy omega-3 fatty acids. For an even better alternative, use canned salmon. It is low in contaminants, high in heart-healthy omega-3s, and sustainably caught in Alaska. You can swap in canned salmon for any canned tuna recipe in this book.

Chicken and vegetable broth: Broth is very versatile because it is super healthy and gives maximum flavor to your cooking.

Herbs and spices: What's the difference? Herbs are the leaves of the plant, and spices are the roots or seeds. For example, cilantro is the leaf and coriander is the seed of the same plant. Cooking with herbs and spices engages the senses. I recommend keeping these in your pantry: red pepper flakes, ground cayenne pepper, smoked paprika, dried thyme, dried basil, dried oregano, and ground cumin.

Panko: Panko is toasted Japanese bread-crumbs. They're larger than regular breadcrumbs and make a crunchy, light batter used in a variety of dishes.

Pasta: I keep a variety of dried pastas in my pantry for quick meals. My favorites are angel-hair pasta, farfalle (bowties), and elbows.

Fresh Staples

These ingredients are perishable, so you'll have to buy them regularly to ensure they are always fresh.

Butter: Unsalted butter has a longer shelf life, about three to four months. Use salted butter for savory dishes, like frittatas and meat, because the sodium will add some flavor. Use unsalted butter for baking, so it does not crash the sweetness.

Basil and cilantro: Fresh basil is known for its aromatic appeal. Basil is the main ingredient in pesto and is often used to add fresh flavor to dishes ranging from sauces to fish. Cilantro adds brightness and is typically added after the dish is cooked.

Dairy products: For some recipes you'll need Greek yogurt, milk or cream, and a variety of cheeses. Parmesan cheese especially—it's one of those magical, flavor-enhancing ingredients, perfect for pasta, soup, or even as a garnish on top of your ravioli. Buy it in a chunk and grate it fresh as needed for the best flavor.

Eggs: They're not just for breakfast! The recipes in this book use large eggs.

Garlic and shallots: Known for its pungent and spicy flavor, garlic usually works in a medium of butter or oil. Sweet and mild shallots add flavor to your sautés and soups and pair well with chicken and fish.

Lemons: Fresh lemons add brightness to dishes with both their juice and zest (the yellow outer part of the peel).

Onions: There are many kinds of onions. In this book I mostly use yellow onions, which give a nice balance of astringency and sweetness to your cooking. You'll also find red onions, which are meatier and are not so sharp when you eat them raw.

Storage Tips

Naturally, you want your food to be delicious, but you also want it to be safe. That means you need to store your ingredients properly to ensure they stay fresh.

Store cooking oils in a cool, dry, and dark place. Olive oil in a beautiful container next to the stove looks nice, but it will go rancid twice as fast as properly stored olive oil.

Buy what you can in bulk for affordability, then store in glass storage containers or jars to keep the food fresh for longer. Dried pasta, for example, can last up to two years if you store it in a cool, dark place.

Carefully wrap, date, and freeze meats. You can also freeze some vegetables, such as broccoli, cauliflower, asparagus, bell peppers, and dark leafy greens. Mixed berries, cherries, pineapple chunks, and bananas also freeze well. Frozen fruits are good for about 12 months; vegetables, for 18 months. Storing them longer is fine, but the quality may decline.

Store your fresh herbs wrapped in a slightly damp paper towel placed in a zip-top plastic bag in the refrigerator.

Place all of your greens in BPA-free bags or bins so they are safe and remain fresh longer.

Organize your produce items in the refrigerator so there is good air circulating around them. Clearly label your ingredients and include their use-by date if you have taken them out of their original packaging. Be sure to check these dates regularly and replace any ingredients that are expired.

Shopping Tips

Fresh foods are not only tastier and healthier; they are also less expensive, ounce for ounce, than processed foods. I recommend buying fresh produce from local farmers' markets or directly from farmers in your area, if possible. If you don't have access to farm-fresh sources, choose the best produce you can find at your local grocery store.

Go with non-GMO (genetically modified organism) foods, if possible. GMO products have had their DNA modified through engineering, and there is a lot of controversy surrounding whether these foods pose health risks. And choose organic when you can, as these foods are free from chemicals.

Here are some tips to keep in mind to keep your weekly grocery shopping fresh and healthy.

- Fresh is always best.

- Frozen is next best. Frozen produce is fresh produce that has been picked at the height of freshness and then quickly frozen. Choose frozen fruit and vegetables that have no additives, such as spices, seasonings, sugar, sauces, or preservatives. All of these are unhealthy and add sodium, fats, and refined sugars to your food.

- Shop the perimeter of the grocery store. This is where the fresh vegetables and fruits are offered. It will also keep you away from the canned foods, which are often loaded up with sodium and sugar.

- Buy your pantry staples from wholesale retailers so you can get discounts on bulk items.

- Inspect every label before placing the item in your cart. Check the ingredients list— just because the package claims that the food is natural, low fat, or healthy doesn't mean it is.

- Select canned fish carefully. Look for wild-caught and organic options. Read the labels, and check out the websites of the food companies.

- Buy lean meats and poultry, and trim them of all visible fat before cooking.

Here are some tips to keep in mind to keep your weekly grocery shopping easy and economical.

- Create a weekly meal plan before you shop, and buy what's on the menu that week.

- Set a time and shop once a week, so you're not rushing and still have the energy to make wise choices when shopping.

- Shop in familiar stores so you will be able to find what you need quickly.

- Plan meals so you have leftovers for lunch the next day.

- Buy only what you need. Just because it's on sale doesn't mean you will use it.

- Supermarket rotisserie chicken is your friend. (Check out chapter 8 if you don't believe me.)

The Best Frozen Produce to Buy

The better you stock your refrigerator, freezer, and pantry, the easier it is to prepare meals. Sometimes getting fresh vegetables is not possible, though. Whether you have run out and couldn't get to the store or the vegetable is not in season, you need a different solution: frozen produce. Here are the staples to keep in your freezer.

Broccoli: If you don't plan on using a whole head of broccoli within a week, frozen broccoli avoids food waste. Typically, it's just the florets, too, which is everyone's favorite part.

Carrots: Frozen carrots can be more nutritious than fresh carrots, as they gain beta-carotene when frozen. Frozen carrots also cost less than fresh carrots.

Cauliflower: Thanks to the snap-freezing process, frozen cauliflower is cheaper to buy and easier to prepare than fresh.

Corn: For the long months when corn is out of season, opt for frozen kernels rather than canned. They are just as sweet as a fresh ear of corn, and they cook in less time.

Mirepoix: This is a mixture of chopped onions, celery, and carrots. It's a staple in many cuisines; the Italians call it soffritto, and in the South it's known as the Holy Trinity. Mirepoix is used as an aromatic flavor base in cooking so many dishes. Recipes in this book use frozen mirepoix to save time.

Peas: Fresh peas can be expensive and are time-consuming to prepare. Frozen peas are a lot simpler to use, and they retain most of their flavor and nutrients when frozen.

About the Recipes

The recipes in this book are rooted in simplicity—a fusion of delicious and bold flavors, using ingredients that are easily found in most grocery stores and farmers' markets. All these recipes use just five ingredients, not counting nonstick cooking spray, oil, water, salt, and pepper. Most take only 30 minutes or less to prepare, cook, and serve, and a lot of them take just 20 minutes or less. The recipes are also structured to make the prepping and cooking process easier. This all saves you time and energy in the kitchen.

At the top of each recipe, you will find an icon telling you what cooking vessel to use (the icons are keyed to the chart on page 5), and a tip if the recipe can also be made in a slow cooker. (If it can, I'll tell you exactly how to adapt it.) You'll see my best estimate of how long it will take you to prepare and cook the dish. You will also find the following labels that will assist you in planning your meals, which is fundamental to a successful and enjoyable experience in the kitchen.

Extra-Quick: These recipes can be prepped, cooked, and served in 20 minutes or less.

Freezer-Friendly: These recipes can be frozen and reheated. I will give you storage and reheating instructions for these.

My goal is to have something for everyone, helping people create indulgent recipes at home using high-quality, fresh ingredients while still keeping dietary restrictions in mind so you will find recipes with the following labels, as well.

- Dairy-Free
- Gluten-Free
- Nut-Free
- Vegan
- Vegetarian

At the end of each recipe, you'll find a helpful little tip.

Cook It Slow: If the recipe can be made in a slow cooker, I'll explain how to adapt it.

Cookware Swap: If a recipe can be prepared in different cookware, I'll tell you how the cooking instructions might change.

From the Freezer: If the recipe is freezer-friendly, I'll give you freezing and reheating instructions.

Ingredient Tip: I'll provide information about an ingredient, such as what to look for when you're buying it, how to store it, or, if it might be unfamiliar, just the basics of what it is.

Prep Tip: I'll give you some inside secrets on how to make prep or cooking easier.

Variation: I'll let you know if one ingredient can be swapped out for another, for variation, convenience, or dietary preference. In some recipes, I'll suggest some extra ingredients you can add to the dish or give you tips on what to do with leftovers.

My wish is that this book becomes a staple in your kitchen, that you will find it helpful and quirky, and that it becomes well loved in your home. The more crumpled the pages, the better. If you have any questions, feel free to reach out to me on my blog at SimplyHealthyish.com. Take the first step to end your dinner struggles tonight. Happy cooking!

Skillet and Sauté Pan

The recipes in this chapter use a skillet or a sauté pan, but what's the difference? They both refer to wide, low-sided pans. While one might be better than the other for a particular recipe, they can generally be used interchangeably—which is great when you don't have space to store several pieces of similar cookware.

A skillet, known more commonly as a frying pan, is ideal for frying, browning, and sautéing chicken, meat, eggs, fish, vegetables, and potatoes. It has low sides that flare out; the lower sides mean it's easier to flip your food. Small, 8-inch skillets are great for making omelets, frittatas, and dishes like shakshuka. A medium, 10-inch skillet is ideal for making evenly cooked fried rice and stir-fries.

A sauté pan has a wide, flat bottom and slightly taller, straight sides. Most home stove burners can comfortably fit a pan of around 12 inches in diameter. Because of its straight sides, a 12-inch sauté pan will also have a large, 12-inch-wide cooking surface.

Besides the different shapes and sizes, you should also consider the material pans are made from. Nonstick, stainless steel, aluminum, and cast iron all have their pros and cons—which is why it's not uncommon to find several types of frying pans in many kitchens.

Seared Salmon with Roasted Corn Salsa, page 29

Here are some things to look for when you're buying a skillet or sauté pan.

Look for triple-layer construction. Triple-layer products usually are made of a layer of aluminum clad between two layers of stainless steel. Aluminum transmits heat very quickly, while stainless steel heats more slowly and maintains its temperature better when cold foods are added to it. Put these two characteristics together, and you've got a pan that heats evenly and maintains its heat for even sautéing and searing. It's also superior for developing fond—the flavorful browned bits that stick to the bottom of the pan after searing that form the base of many pan sauces.

Avoid disk-bottomed pans. Disk-bottomed pans are stainless steel pans with an aluminum disk welded to the bottom. Conceptually, they work the same way as triple-layer products, but the disks have a tendency to fall off and don't distribute heat to the edges of the pan.

Look for riveted handles. Welded handles fall off with repeated use. Riveted handles should last a lifetime.

If it's your first pan, don't buy nonstick. A nonstick pan is great for some uses—eggs, pancakes, super delicate fish—but a stainless steel pan is far more versatile. It can withstand very high heat (which nonstick cannot), giving you a better sear.

Here are some things to remember when you're cooking in a skillet or sauté pan.

- **Your skillet must be hot enough** for ingredients to sizzle or create a crust. Otherwise your food will stick to the pan and won't brown.

- Cooking in a good skillet or sauté pan uses just a little oil and cooks the food quickly, so **cut your vegetables into small, even-size pieces.** Start with the vegetables that need the longest cooking and keep stirring.

- **If you are adding a sauce, do it at the very end**, then toss to coat and serve right away.

Skillet Ravioli in Marinara Sauce

NUT-FREE · VEGETARIAN

Pasta is an obvious choice for quick meals, but plain pasta in sauce isn't the most satisfying meal. Using store-bought ravioli, though, turns it into a dish you can really sink your teeth into. You can use any type of ravioli you like—stuffed with meat, if you want, or mushrooms, veggies, or cheese for a vegetarian version.

SERVES 4
PREP TIME: 5 MINUTES
COOK TIME: 20 MINUTES

1 tablespoon extra-virgin olive oil

1 small onion, diced

1 (24-ounce) jar marinara sauce

1 cup water

Salt

Freshly ground black pepper

1 (20-ounce) package fresh ravioli

⅓ cup chopped fresh basil

½ cup grated Parmesan cheese

1. In the skillet over medium-high heat, heat the olive oil. Add the onion and sauté until it turns soft and translucent, about 7 minutes.

2. Pour in the marinara sauce and water, and season with salt and pepper. Bring to a boil, and stir in the ravioli. Reduce the heat and simmer for about 6 minutes, or until the ravioli is soft and cooked through.

3. To serve, scatter the chopped basil and Parmesan cheese on top.

INGREDIENT TIP: Shopping for marinara sauce can be confusing, especially with so many brands out there, so compare the nutrition labels before you buy. Look for a sauce that has no more than 2 to 3 grams of saturated fat per serving and no more than 4 grams of sugar per serving. Be cautious about sodium. Most store-bought sauces are very high in sodium, and some are sky-high. Look for a sauce with no more than 450 milligrams per serving—the lower, the better. My favorites include Newman's Own, Amy's, Prego, and Rao's.

PER SERVING Calories: 250; Total Fat: 11g; Saturated Fat: 5g; Cholesterol: 13mg; Sodium: 1,728mg; Total Carbohydrates: 28g; Sugars: 11g; Protein: 12g

Vegetable Quesadilla

NUT-FREE · VEGETARIAN

Sautéing veggies to add to your quesadillas adds only a few minutes to the prep and cooking time, but it really cranks up the flavor factor—not to mention adding a ton of nutrients, too. This recipe transforms your run-of-the-mill quesadilla from a quick snack to a healthy dinner.

SERVES 3
PREP TIME: 5 MINUTES
COOK TIME: 25 MINUTES

1 tablespoon extra-virgin olive oil

1 cup chopped bell peppers, any colors

½ cup thinly sliced mushrooms

¼ cup thinly sliced red onion

6 (9-inch) flour tortillas

1½ cups shredded Mexican cheese blend

1. In the skillet over medium-high heat, heat the olive oil. Add the bell peppers, mushrooms, and onion and cook for about 5 minutes, or until just tender. Set aside.

2. Place 1 tortilla in the pan. Sprinkle about ¼ cup of cheese over the tortilla, and top with a third of the vegetable mixture. Sprinkle with another ¼ cup of cheese, then top with 1 more tortilla. Cook until golden on both sides, about 2 to 3 minutes on each side.

3. Remove from the pan and cut into triangles with a pizza cutter. Repeat the process two more times with the remaining tortillas, cheese, and vegetables, and serve.

VARIATION: For a different flavor, you can replace ½ cup of the chopped bell peppers with ½ cup chopped zucchini—or whatever other vegetable you like that's in season.

PER SERVING Calories: 539; Total Fat: 30g; Saturated Fat: 13g; Cholesterol: 50mg; Sodium: 1,182mg; Total Carbohydrates: 54g; Sugars: 3g; Protein: 21g

Caramelized Onion and Potato Frittata

GLUTEN-FREE · NUT-FREE · VEGETARIAN

Eggs are a go-to in my house for quick, delicious meals. They're endlessly versatile, and I always have them on hand. This caramelized onion and potato frittata is an easy way to turn eggs into a hearty dinner. It is vegetarian, but so full of flavor that no one will feel like they're missing out.

SERVES 2
PREP TIME: 5 MINUTES
COOK TIME: 25 MINUTES

1 tablespoon extra-virgin olive oil

1 medium russet potato, unpeeled, thinly sliced

1 teaspoon crushed garlic

1 small onion, thinly sliced

4 eggs, whisked

Salt

½ cup shredded cheddar cheese

1. In the skillet over medium heat, heat the olive oil. Add the potato, garlic, and onion, and cook for 15 minutes, until the potato is nearly soft.

2. In a medium bowl, combine the eggs and salt. Pour into the pan, and sprinkle with the cheddar cheese. Reduce the heat to low, cover, and cook for 7 minutes, until the top is set, and serve.

PREP TIP: Thinly slicing potatoes can be frustrating. Try using a mandoline slicer or potato peeler for a better result. Be sure to use the mandoline guard and pay close attention.

PER SERVING Calories: 403; Total Fat: 25g; Saturated Fat: 10g; Cholesterol: 357mg; Sodium: 383mg; Total Carbohydrates: 24g; Sugars: 3g; Protein: 21g

 # Tex-Mex Omelet

GLUTEN-FREE · NUT-FREE · VEGETARIAN

I love cooking omelets because they take just a few minutes to cook and you can fill them with infinite combinations of tasty fillings. This Tex-Mex version is loaded up with sweet potato, bell pepper, black beans, and cheese. If you like a spicy kick, use pepper Jack cheese or top it with your favorite salsa.

SERVES 2
PREP TIME: 5 MINUTES
COOK TIME: 25 MINUTES

1 tablespoon extra-virgin olive oil

1 medium sweet potato, unpeeled, finely diced

1 small green bell pepper, seeded and diced

½ cup canned black beans, rinsed and drained

Salt

Freshly ground black pepper

4 eggs, whisked

½ cup Monterey Jack cheese

1. In the skillet over medium-high heat, heat the olive oil. Add the sweet potato and cook until nearly soft, about 10 minutes.

2. Add the bell pepper, and cook for another 5 minutes. Add the black beans, and cook for 1 minute. Season with salt and pepper.

3. Pour in the eggs, and sprinkle with the cheese. Cook until the eggs are set, 3 to 4 minutes, and serve.

INGREDIENT TIP: When buying sweet potatoes, look for small or medium ones. They taste creamier than larger sweet potatoes. Also, always look for a darker skin color—an indication that the potato is richer in the antioxidant beta-carotene.

PER SERVING Calories: 419; Total Fat: 25g; Saturated Fat: 9g; Cholesterol: 353mg; Sodium: 375mg; Total Carbohydrates: 27g; Sugars: 8g; Protein: 24g

Shakshuka

8-INCH SKILLET

DAIRY-FREE · GLUTEN-FREE · NUT-FREE · VEGETARIAN

Shakshuka—eggs poached in a spicy tomato sauce—is popular in several Mediterranean cuisines. It has been a favorite in my family for many decades. This take on it gets smoky flavor by using fire-roasted tomatoes and makes a stunning weeknight supper. A loaf of crusty bread is the perfect accompaniment—you'll want it for sopping up all that yummy sauce.

SERVES 4
PREP TIME: 10 MINUTES
COOK TIME: 15 MINUTES

2 tablespoons extra-virgin olive oil

1 onion, halved and thinly sliced

4 cups stemmed and chopped kale

¼ teaspoon ground oregano

Salt

Freshly ground black pepper

1 (15-ounce) can fire-roasted diced tomatoes, drained

4 eggs

1. In the skillet over medium heat, heat the olive oil. Add the onion and cook for 5 minutes, until soft.

2. Stir in the kale and oregano, and season with salt and pepper. Cook, stirring often, until the kale is wilted and tender, about 2 minutes. Add the tomatoes and bring to a simmer.

3. Make four indentations in the mixture, and crack an egg into each one. Cook, uncovered, until the whites are set and the egg yolks are still runny, about 5 minutes, and serve.

PREP TIP: Put your onion in the freezer for 30 minutes just before cutting it to prevent those onion tears.

PER SERVING Calories: 180; Total Fat: 11g; Saturated Fat: 2g; Cholesterol: 164mg; Sodium: 255mg; Total Carbohydrates: 13g; Sugars: 6g; Protein: 8g

Canadian Bacon and Mushroom Frittata

8-INCH SKILLET

DAIRY-FREE · GLUTEN-FREE · NUT-FREE

Frittata is one of those rare dishes that can be enjoyed hot out of the oven but is still delicious at room temperature or even straight out of the refrigerator. I love to make one for dinner and then enjoy the leftovers for breakfast, lunch, or another dinner later in the week. This one is especially satisfying since it has both Canadian bacon and lots of vegetables.

SERVES 4
PREP TIME: 10 MINUTES
COOK TIME: 20 MINUTES

1 tablespoon extra-virgin olive oil

4 Canadian bacon slices, diced small

1 red bell pepper, seeded and diced

8 ounces cremini mushrooms, thinly sliced

3 cups baby spinach

4 eggs, whisked

Salt

Freshly ground black pepper

1. In the skillet over medium heat, heat the olive oil. Add the bacon and bell pepper and cook for 7 minutes.

2. Add the mushrooms and spinach, and cook for 3 minutes.

3. In a medium bowl, combine the eggs, salt, and pepper. Pour into the pan. Reduce the heat to low, cover, and cook for 7 minutes, until the top is set, and serve.

PREP TIP: Mushrooms absorb water, so to clean them, lightly moisten a paper towel with cool water and wipe them before cooking.

PER SERVING Calories: 212; Total Fat: 12g; Saturated Fat: 3g; Cholesterol: 192mg; Sodium: 925mg; Total Carbohydrates: 7g; Sugars: 1g; Protein: 20g

Cauliflower Fried Rice

SAUTÉ PAN

DAIRY-FREE · NUT-FREE

Cauliflower fried rice is the perfect simple weeknight side dish. With the succulent flavors of the pork loin and the rich umami of the soy sauce, you have a wonderful, lighter spin on classic fried rice. Best of all, it is low-carb and can easily be made vegan.

SERVES 4
PREP TIME: 10 MINUTES
COOK TIME: 20 MINUTES

2 tablespoons extra-virgin olive oil, divided

2 cups cubed boneless pork loin

2 garlic cloves, minced

1 cup frozen mixed peas and carrots

3 cups grated fresh cauliflower

3 tablespoons soy sauce

Optional garnish:

2 scallions, thinly sliced

1. In the sauté pan over medium-high heat, heat 1 tablespoon of olive oil. Cook the pork loin until slightly browned and cooked through, about 7 minutes. Transfer to a plate and set aside.

2. In the same pan over medium heat, heat the remaining 1 tablespoon of olive oil. Sauté the garlic for 2 minutes.

3. Move the garlic to one side of the pan. Add the pork loin and peas and carrots, and cook until the vegetables begin to soften, about 3 minutes.

4. Stir in the cauliflower and soy sauce. Stir-fry until the mixture is slightly browned, about 5 minutes. Garnish with scallions, if using, and serve.

VARIATION: You can substitute any lean meat, or tofu if you are a vegetarian, for the pork loin. If you are not a fan of soy sauce, try tamari. It has a similar flavor but is gluten-free and vegan.

PER SERVING Calories: 190; Total Fat: 11g; Saturated Fat: 3g; Cholesterol: 27mg; Sodium: 928mg; Total Carbohydrates: 11g; Sugars: 1g; Protein: 14g

Mu Shu Pork Tacos

EXTRA-QUICK · DAIRY-FREE · NUT-FREE

This recipe combines two of my favorite quick-cooking cuisines—Chinese and Mexican—in one simple and delicious dish. Serve this family style with the tortillas on the side and let diners make their own wraps. Pass a store-bought hoisin sauce for drizzling over the filling for even more flavor.

SERVES 4
PREP TIME: 10 MINUTES
COOK TIME: 10 MINUTES

3 tablespoons extra-virgin olive oil

1 cup sliced shiitake mushroom caps

12 ounces boneless pork shoulder, trimmed and thinly sliced

2 tablespoons soy sauce

Salt

Freshly ground black pepper

4 cups thinly sliced lettuce leaves

8 (6-inch) flour tortillas

Optional garnish:

2 scallions, thinly sliced

1. In the skillet over high heat, heat the oil. Add the mushrooms and cook until just tender, about 4 minutes.

2. Add the pork and cook, stirring occasionally, until the pork is browned, about 4 minutes. Add the soy sauce, and season with salt and pepper. Cook until heated through.

3. Spread the lettuce over one half of each tortilla, then top with pork and mushroom mixture and garnish with scallions, if using. Fold the uncovered half over, and serve.

VARIATION: You can use spinach or corn tortillas for this recipe.

PER SERVING Calories: 317; Total Fat: 15g; Saturated Fat: 3g; Cholesterol: 49mg; Sodium: 565mg; Total Carbohydrates: 29g; Sugars: 1g; Protein: 19g

Classic Burger

10-INCH SKILLET

EXTRA-QUICK · DAIRY-FREE · NUT-FREE

The humble hamburger is one of the easiest, tastiest meals you can cook. Every home cook should know how to make a good classic burger, and this is one of the best. To make a quality burger, you want to start with high-quality ground beef with a good amount of fat because that's what makes it juicy and delicious. I recommend using beef that is 80 percent lean, 20 percent fat.

SERVES 4
PREP TIME: 5 MINUTES
COOK TIME: 15 MINUTES

1 pound 80/20 ground beef

Salt

Freshly ground black pepper

2 tablespoons extra-virgin olive oil

4 hamburger buns, toasted

1 beefsteak tomato, thinly sliced

1 onion, sliced

1. Shape the ground beef into four patties. Flatten with the palm of your hand so they are slightly wider in diameter than the buns. Season generously with salt and pepper.

2. In the skillet over high heat, heat the olive oil. Sear two burger patties in the hot skillet, being careful not to burn them (3 minutes on each side for medium-rare). Do not press down on the burgers, as this will release their juices and make them dry. Repeat with the remaining two burgers.

3. Serve the burgers on the toasted buns with the slices of tomato and onion.

VARIATION: On a low-carb diet or gluten-free? Simply replace the hamburger buns with lettuce leaves.

PER SERVING Calories: 489; Total Fat: 32g; Saturated Fat: 11g; Cholesterol: 80mg; Sodium: 323mg; Total Carbohydrates: 26g; Sugars: 2g; Protein: 24g

 # Tuna Patties

DAIRY-FREE • NUT-FREE

I always keep cans of tuna in the pantry because they can be turned into a number of easy dinners. These tuna patties are one of my favorite go-to recipes because they're easy, flavorful and use ingredients that I pretty much always have in the kitchen. Serving them over lightly dressed salad greens makes it a nice, fresh-tasting meal.

SERVES 4
PREP TIME: 5 MINUTES
COOK TIME: 20 MINUTES

2 (5-ounce) cans tuna, drained, liquid reserved

1 egg

¼ cup finely chopped onion

½ cup panko breadcrumbs

Salt

Freshly ground black pepper

4 tablespoons extra-virgin olive oil, divided

4 cups mixed salad greens, such as arugula, romaine, and spinach

Optional garnish:

1 lemon, cut into wedges

1. In a large bowl, mix the tuna, egg, onion, and breadcrumbs, and season with salt and pepper. Use your hands to form the mixture into four patties. If it is too dry, add a little liquid from the canned tuna.

2. In the skillet over medium heat, heat 2 tablespoons of oil. Add two patties and brown on both sides (4 to 5 minutes per side). Drain on paper towels and set aside. Repeat with the remaining two patties.

3. In a large serving bowl, combine the mixed greens with the remaining 2 tablespoons of oil, and season with salt and pepper. Place the tuna patties on top, squeeze the lemon wedges over top, if using, and serve.

INGREDIENT TIP: When buying canned tuna, always look for environmentally sustainable options. In general, skipjack (light) tuna is less overfished than albacore (white) tuna. The website seafoodwatch.org is a great resource to check whether a fish is sustainable. It also has an app that can help you make a good, sustainable choice while shopping.

PER SERVING Calories: 265; Total Fat: 16g; Saturated Fat: 3g; Cholesterol: 66mg; Sodium: 149mg; Total Carbohydrates: 7g; Sugars: 1g; Protein: 25g

Pan-Grilled Shrimp Salad

EXTRA-QUICK · DAIRY-FREE · GLUTEN-FREE · NUT-FREE

Here's the thing about this recipe: It's so easy to make. It's also incredibly flavorful and will meet all of your spring salad cravings. You can mix the arugula with any of your favorite salad greens, such as baby spinach and butter lettuce.

SERVES 3
PREP TIME: 10 MINUTES
COOK TIME: 10 MINUTES

4 tablespoons extra-virgin olive oil, divided

12 fresh or frozen jumbo shrimp, peeled and deveined, thawed if frozen

Salt

Freshly ground black pepper

2 to 3 cups arugula

Zest and juice of 1 lemon

1. Preheat the skillet over medium-high heat, and add 2 table-spoons of olive oil. Add the shrimp, season with salt and pepper, and sear for about 3 minutes on each side, until pink, opaque, and cooked through. Set aside.

2. In a large bowl, toss the arugula with the lemon zest, lemon juice, and the remaining 2 tablespoons of olive oil, and season with salt and pepper. Serve the shrimp over the salad.

INGREDIENT TIP: I always keep a bag of shrimp in my freezer, because I never know when I'll need them. If you need to thaw your shrimp right away, place them in a colander in the sink and run cold water over them for about 5 minutes.

PER SERVING Calories: 262; Total Fat: 20g; Saturated Fat: 3g; Cholesterol: 160mg; Sodium: 772mg; Total Carbohydrates: 2g; Sugars: 0g; Protein: 18g

Tilapia Tacos

DAIRY-FREE · GLUTEN-FREE · NUT-FREE

Taco night gets a fresh, healthy makeover with these fish tacos. This recipe hits all the right notes: savory Mexican flavors, fresh veggies, spicy salsa, and succulent, pan-seared fish fillets that cook up in just a few minutes. I could happily eat this every Tuesday.

SERVES 4
PREP TIME: 15 MINUTES
COOK TIME: 15 MINUTES

1 teaspoon ground cumin

Dash salt

Dash freshly ground black pepper

8 (1- to 1½-pound) tilapia fillets

2 tablespoons extra-virgin olive oil

8 corn tortilla shells

1 cup finely chopped red cabbage

1 cup store-bought salsa

Optional garnish:

¼ cup chopped fresh cilantro

¼ cup chopped jalapeño

1. In a small bowl, mix the cumin, salt, and pepper. Rub the spice mixture onto both sides of the tilapia fillets.

2. In the skillet, warm the tortillas for about 30 seconds on medium-low heat on each side. Set aside.

3. In the same skillet, over medium-high heat, heat the olive oil. Working in batches, panfry the tilapia for 2 to 3 minutes on each side, until white, opaque, and cooked through. Set aside. To serve, divide the fish evenly among the tortillas. Top with cabbage and salsa, and garnish with fresh cilantro and jalapeño, if using.

INGREDIENT TIP: When buying store-bought salsa, always check the expiration date for a better quality. Once opened, salsa will keep in the refrigerator for 1 to 2 weeks. Some salsas can have an excess of sodium, which is of particular concern if you're watching your heart health. Always check the nutrition label.

PER SERVING Calories: 391; Total Fat: 11g; Saturated Fat: 1g; Cholesterol: 200mg; Sodium: 384mg; Total Carbohydrates: 28g; Sugars: 4g; Protein: 47g

Seared Salmon with Roasted Corn Salsa

10-INCH SKILLET · DUTCH OVEN

DAIRY-FREE · GLUTEN-FREE · NUT-FREE

I love salmon for easy dinners because it's so flavorful on its own. But let's face it, even salmon gets boring. This pan-seared version is hardly any more trouble to make, and the quick corn salsa gives it tons of bright, fresh flavor. If you don't have basil, feel free to substitute with other fresh herbs, like cilantro or oregano.

SERVES 4
PREP TIME: 10 MINUTES
COOK TIME: 20 MINUTES

5 tablespoons extra-virgin olive oil, divided

3 cups frozen corn, thawed

4 (5-ounce) skin-on salmon fillets

Salt

Freshly ground black pepper

1 cup diced onion

½ cup chopped fresh basil

¼ cup red wine vinegar

1. In the skillet over medium-high heat, heat 1 tablespoon of oil. Add the corn and cook for 10 to 12 minutes, or until the corn starts to brown, stirring occasionally. Set aside.

2. Over medium-high heat, add 2 tablespoons of olive oil to the skillet. Season the salmon with salt and pepper. Cook the salmon skin-side down for 3 to 4 minutes, or until the skin is crispy. Flip, then cook for another 4 minutes on the other side, until the fish is opaque and flakes easily with a fork.

3. In a medium bowl, combine the onion, roasted corn, basil, the remaining 2 tablespoons of olive oil, and the red wine vinegar. Season with salt and pepper.

4. Serve the salmon skin-side up with the roasted corn salsa on the side.

COOKWARE SWAP: You can use a 5.5-quart Dutch oven to cook this recipe, and you don't need to change a thing.

INGREDIENT TIP: For perfectly cooked and crispy salmon skin, always use fillets at room temperature and a skillet over high heat.

PER SERVING Calories: 522; Total Fat: 34g; Saturated Fat: 6g; Cholesterol: 85mg; Sodium: 144mg; Total Carbohydrates: 24g; Sugars: 5g; Protein: 32g

Mom's Turkey Hash

DAIRY-FREE • GLUTEN-FREE • NUT-FREE

Sometimes I just want breakfast for dinner. When that happens, I always make this turkey hash. It's colorful and nutritious, and makes a delicious dinner. I have been enjoying this meal since my mom used to make it when I was a child. I have put my own spin on it since then by adding ground cumin, and the result is delicious.

SERVES 4
PREP TIME: 10 MINUTES
COOK TIME: 15 MINUTES

4 tablespoons extra-virgin olive oil, divided

1 medium onion, diced

1 cup diced bell pepper, any colors

2 large sweet potatoes, unpeeled, diced

2 cups diced cooked turkey breast

1 teaspoon ground cumin

Salt

Freshly ground black pepper

1. In the skillet over medium-high heat, heat 2 tablespoons of olive oil. Add the onion and bell pepper and cook until slightly soft and brown, 3 to 4 minutes.

2. Add the remaining 2 tablespoons of oil and the sweet potatoes, and cook for 10 minutes, then press with a spatula to flatten into an even layer. Cook until the sweet potatoes are browned on the bottom. If they're too dry, add a splash of water.

3. Add the turkey and stir into a hash. Season with the cumin, salt, and pepper, and serve.

COOKWARE SWAP: You can use a 5.5-quart Dutch oven to cook this recipe, and you don't need to change a thing.

PER SERVING Calories: 289; Total Fat: 16g; Saturated Fat: 2g; Cholesterol: 45mg; Sodium: 724mg; Total Carbohydrates: 20g; Sugars: 5g; Protein: 17g

Black Pepper Chicken Sandwich

DAIRY-FREE • NUT-FREE

Boneless chicken breast is a great protein for quick dinners because it cooks fast and its mild flavor pairs with just about any flavor profile. For this sandwich, it's stir-fried with onion, soy sauce, and a hearty dose of black pepper. Fresh cucumber and cilantro give the sandwich crunch and a nice, fresh flavor.

SERVES 4
PREP TIME: 10 MINUTES
COOK TIME: 15 MINUTES

1 tablespoon extra-virgin olive oil

1 small onion, finely sliced

1 pound boneless, skinless chicken breast, cut into bite-size pieces

2 teaspoons soy sauce

1 teaspoon freshly ground black pepper

4 soft French rolls, split and lightly toasted

Optional garnish:

1 cup fresh cilantro

1 small cucumber, thinly sliced

1. In the skillet over medium-high heat, heat the olive oil. Add the onion and cook for 3 minutes. Add the chicken and soy sauce and stir-fry for 5 minutes. Add the pepper, and continue cooking until the meat is cooked, 2 to 3 minutes more.

2. Divide the chicken pieces and onion among the rolls, placing them on one side of each roll. Add the cilantro and cucumber, if using, close up the sandwiches, and serve.

VARIATION: Don't feel like having a sandwich tonight? Simply serve the chicken over steamed instant rice.

PER SERVING Calories: 340; Total Fat: 8g; Saturated Fat: 1g; Cholesterol: 65mg; Sodium: 595mg; Total Carbohydrates: 35g; Sugars: 5g; Protein: 32g

 # Thai Lettuce Wraps

8-INCH SKILLET

EXTRA-QUICK · DAIRY-FREE · NUT-FREE

This simple chicken stir-fry gets Thai flavor from garlic and lots of fresh basil. Serving it in lettuce cups makes it a satisfying low-carb meal, but you can add steamed rice if you like. Chop up a hot pepper, like jalapeño or serrano, and add it with the chicken for the spicy kick you find in many Thai dishes.

SERVES 4
PREP TIME: 10 MINUTES
COOK TIME: 10 MINUTES

1 butter lettuce head

1 tablespoon extra-virgin olive oil

4 garlic cloves, roughly chopped

½ pound ground chicken

2 tablespoons soy sauce

Salt

Freshly ground black pepper

1 cup fresh Thai basil leaves

Optional garnish:

Fresh cilantro

Thinly sliced carrots

¼ cup chopped peanuts

1. Carefully separate the head of lettuce, so you have lettuce cups.

2. In the skillet over medium-high heat, heat the olive oil. Add the garlic and cook for 2 minutes. Add the chicken and cook, breaking up the meat with a wooden spoon, until cooked through, about 5 minutes. Add the soy sauce, and season with salt and pepper. Add the basil leaves and cook for another 30 seconds, until they are just fragrant.

3. Spoon the chicken mixture into the lettuce cups, top with the cilantro, carrots, and peanuts, if using, and serve.

INGREDIENT TIP: To store butter lettuce cups in the refrigerator for a few days, wash the leaves and wrap them in paper towels, then seal in a plastic bag.

PER SERVING Calories: 130; Total Fat: 8g; Saturated Fat: 2g; Cholesterol: 48mg; Sodium: 528mg; Total Carbohydrates: 4g; Sugars: 1g; Protein: 11g

Skillet Chicken and Asparagus

EXTRA-QUICK · DAIRY-FREE · GLUTEN-FREE · NUT-FREE

This is my favorite weeknight dish. It is so easy to prepare, and you'll love how flavorful the chicken breasts are, especially with the balsamic reduction and cherry tomatoes adding sweet and savory flavor.

SERVES 4
PREP TIME: 5 MINUTES
COOK TIME: 15 MINUTES

2 tablespoons extra-virgin olive oil

4 boneless, skinless chicken breasts

Salt

Freshly ground black pepper

1 pound asparagus, trimmed

3 cups cherry tomatoes, halved

2 tablespoons chopped fresh basil

2 tablespoons balsamic reduction

1. In the skillet over medium-low heat, heat the olive oil. Sprinkle the chicken generously with salt and pepper on all sides. Add the chicken and asparagus to the hot pan and cook for 8 minutes per side, or until the chicken is no longer pink in the middle.

2. In a large bowl, combine the tomatoes, basil, and balsamic reduction, and season with salt and pepper. Toss well, spoon over the cooked chicken, and serve.

INGREDIENT TIP: A balsamic vinegar reduction is concentrated and thickened balsamic vinegar; it's made by cooking down the vinegar until it has reduced. You can find it near the balsamic vinegar in the grocery store. To make a balsamic reduction at home, combine 1 cup balsamic vinegar with 3 tablespoons honey in a small saucepan. Bring to a boil and immediately reduce the heat to low. Let it simmer for 20 minutes, until the sauce is reduced by about half and is a thick consistency.

PER SERVING Calories: 257; Total Fat: 9g; Saturated Fat: 1g; Cholesterol: 65mg; Sodium: 123mg; Total Carbohydrates: 18g; Sugars: 12g; Protein: 30g

Noodle Stir-Fry

10-INCH SKILLET · SAUTÉ PAN

EXTRA-QUICK · DAIRY-FREE · NUT-FREE

Noodles are always welcome after a long day. This version is studded with chicken and mushrooms with savory Asian flavors. It is hearty comfort food that can be on the table in less than 30 minutes, so you can bet it's a favorite in my house.

SERVES 4 to 6
PREP TIME: 10 MINUTES
COOK TIME: 10 MINUTES

1 pound fresh noodles, preferably yakisoba noodles

2 tablespoons extra-virgin olive oil

12 ounces boneless, skinless chicken breast, cut into ½-inch-thick slices

2 small garlic cloves, minced

1 cup sliced button mushrooms

3 tablespoons soy sauce

Optional garnish:

1 tablespoon chopped scallions

1. Open the package of noodles, and loosen them in a large bowl. Separate any strands that are clumped together.

2. In the skillet or pan over medium heat, heat the oil. Add the chicken, spread it out, and cook until lightly browned, about 3 minutes. Add the garlic and mushrooms and cook for 15 seconds.

3. Add the noodles, and spread them around using tongs. Cook for about 3 minutes.

4. Add the soy sauce to the pan. Continue tossing until everything is combined, about 2 minutes. Garnish with the scallions, if using, and serve.

INGREDIENT TIP: I use Fortune Yaki-Soba Japanese Style Stir Fry Noodles, which are commonly available at many grocery stores. You can also replace them with fresh Hong Kong (chow mein) noodles, wonton noodles, Chinese egg noodles, lo mein, or ramen. For a healthier meal, you can use a spiralizer or veggie peeler to make zucchini noodles.

PER SERVING Calories: 545; Total Fat: 9g; Saturated Fat: 1g; Cholesterol: 49mg; Sodium: 1,637mg; Total Carbohydrates: 87g; Sugars: 1g; Protein: 37g

Chicken Marsala Pasta

SAUTÉ PAN

DAIRY-FREE · NUT-FREE

Marsala wine gives this pasta dish classic Italian flavor. If you don't have it, you can substitute a dry white wine with a splash of brandy or a light red wine, like a pinot noir. The flavor will be different, but it will still be tasty.

SERVES 4 to 6
PREP TIME: 10 MINUTES
COOK TIME: 25 MINUTES

4 boneless, skinless chicken breasts, cubed

Salt

Freshly ground black pepper

3 tablespoons extra-virgin olive oil, divided

2 shallots, thinly sliced

1 cup chicken broth

1 cup Marsala wine

1 pound dried fettuccine

Optional garnish:

⅓ cup chopped fresh parsley

1. Season the chicken with salt and pepper. In the sauté pan over medium-low heat, heat 2 tablespoons of oil. Add the chicken and cook for 5 minutes on each side, until golden brown. Set aside.

2. Add the remaining 1 tablespoon of oil and the shallots to the pan, and sauté for 4 to 5 minutes. Add the chicken broth and wine, and scrape the bottom with a wooden spoon to remove any browned bits. Turn the heat to low, then add the pasta. Season with salt and pepper. Cook until the pasta is al dente (firm to the bite), about 10 minutes.

3. Return the chicken to the pan. Garnish with the chopped parsley, if using, and serve immediately.

PREP TIP: For restaurant-quality texture on the chicken, dredge the breasts in ½ cup all-purpose flour before putting them in the skillet.

PER SERVING Calories: 691; Total Fat: 14g; Saturated Fat: 2g; Cholesterol: 65mg; Sodium: 314mg; Total Carbohydrates: 87g; Sugars: 4g; Protein: 62g

Saucepan and Stockpot

Whether you're cooking hard-boiled eggs, heating soup, or warming up last night's leftovers, a saucepan is your pot of choice. Don't let its name deceive you—a saucepan is a pot. Saucepan sizes are based on their capacity; they range in size from around 2 cups to 16 cups. Most saucepans have straight sides and are a medium depth. Usually, they come with a cover that fits tightly inside the rim of the pot. The recipes in this chapter use a 2-quart saucepan.

Stockpots are used to make broth or stock, which is often used as a base for recipes, and can also be used to boil pasta or steam vegetables. They are taller than saucepans and have straight sides and a tight-fitting cover. The recipes in this chapter use a 5.5-quart stockpot.

Buying a good saucepan or stockpot is important because they have so many uses. Here are some things to look for when buying and using a saucepan or stockpot.

Sweet Potato Thai Curry Soup, page 48

- When cooking acidic foods, such as toma-toes, lemons, or cranberries, you want to use a **nonreactive pot**, such as stainless steel, enamel coated, or ceramic. Reactive pans, such as aluminum and cast iron, can impart an odd color and/or a metallic flavor to acidic foods.

- **Thick, heavy-bottomed pots** help prevent burning. For example, soup requires time to cook, so the pot will be sitting on the stove top for a long time. A thick, heavy-bottomed pot will ensure your soup does not stick or burn.

- Look for soup pots that have **handles securely attached** with heavy screws or rivets. Welded handles will fall off with repeated use, which could be disastrous if you are carrying a full pot of soup when it happens.

- Don't leave your boiled vegetables for too long in a pot of hot water, because they will continue to cook even with the heat turned off. Instead, **stop the cooking process** by plunging your cooked vegetables into an ice water bath or running them under cold water.

Chicken Noodle Soup

DAIRY-FREE · NUT-FREE

There's just something comforting about a bowl of homemade chicken noodle soup on a rainy day! You know what I'm talking about—the hearty, tastes-like-Mom's-cooking flavors that put a smile on your face no matter what sort of day you've had. Make this with any pasta shape, from elbows to bowties.

SERVES 4
PREP TIME: 10 MINUTES
COOK TIME: 20 MINUTES

2 tablespoons extra-virgin olive oil

2 cups frozen mirepoix

2 cups diced cooked chicken breast

½ cup your favorite dried pasta shape

6 cups chicken broth

Salt

Freshly ground black pepper

1. In the stockpot over medium heat, heat the olive oil. Add the mirepoix and cook for 5 minutes. Add the chicken, pasta, and broth. Season with salt and pepper, and bring to a boil.

2. Simmer for 10 minutes, or until the pasta is cooked, and serve.

INGREDIENT TIP: Mirepoix is a combination of onions, celery, and carrots. To make your own, combine equal parts of all three finely diced ingredients.

PER SERVING Calories: 272; Total Fat: 11g; Saturated Fat: 2g; Cholesterol: 52mg; Sodium: 1,233mg; Total Carbohydrates: 11g; Sugars: 2g; Protein: 29g

Quick Minestrone

DAIRY-FREE · NUT-FREE

Minestrone is well known as a soup that's chock-full of ingredients—pasta, beans, and lots of vegetables. Using a frozen mirepoix (a mix of diced onions, celery, and carrots) instead of fresh saves time and gets a ton of flavor into this soup without all that peeling and dicing.

SERVES 4
PREP TIME: 10 MINUTES
COOK TIME: 20 MINUTES

1 cup dried cavatappi, rotini, or elbow macaroni

2 cups frozen mirepoix

6 cups chicken broth

1 (14.5-ounce) can diced tomatoes

1 (16-ounce) can kidney beans, rinsed and drained

Salt

Freshly ground black pepper

Optional garnish:

2 tablespoons grated Parmesan cheese

1. In the stockpot, combine the pasta, mirepoix, broth, tomatoes with their juices, and beans, and season with salt and pepper. Bring to a boil, and reduce to low heat. Simmer for 10 minutes.

2. Ladle the soup into bowls. Sprinkle the Parmesan cheese on top, if using, and serve.

PREP TIP: Be sure to rinse canned beans under cool, running water as this can reduce the sodium content by about 40 percent.

PER SERVING Calories: 321; Total Fat: 3g; Saturated Fat: 1g; Cholesterol: 0mg; Sodium: 1,552mg; Total Carbohydrates: 52g; Sugars: 10g; Protein: 20g

Rice Noodle Soup

DAIRY-FREE · NUT-FREE · VEGAN

This noodle soup, with thin rice noodles served in a savory broth flavored with garlic and soy sauce, is great for when you need a comforting meal. Add chopped fresh herbs, like basil, cilantro, and mint, for even more flavor.

SERVES 4
PREP TIME: 10 MINUTES
COOK TIME: 15 MINUTES

1 tablespoon extra-virgin olive oil

3 garlic cloves, minced

4 cups vegetable broth

2 cups water

3 tablespoons soy sauce

7 ounces thin rice noodles (rice vermicelli)

4 baby bok choy heads, chopped

1. In the stockpot over high heat, heat the olive oil. Add the garlic and cook for 30 seconds.

2. Add the broth, water, and soy sauce, and bring to a boil.

3. Add the rice noodles and bok choy and cook for 3 to 4 minutes, until the noodles are cooked through, and serve.

VARIATION: You can substitute pad Thai rice noodles and use chicken broth. If you don't like or can't find bok choy, you can substitute 3 ounces (about 2 cups) spinach.

PER SERVING Calories: 250; Total Fat: 4g; Saturated Fat: 1g; Cholesterol: 0mg; Sodium: 1,372mg; Total Carbohydrates: 47g; Sugars: 3g; Protein: 6g

 # Tofu Noodle Soup

DAIRY-FREE • NUT-FREE

Frozen mirepoix, store-bought chicken broth, and instant ramen noodles make this ramen soup a great quick-fix dinner. Diced tofu gives it texture and a big protein boost, making it a filling meal.

SERVES 4
PREP TIME: 10 MINUTES
COOK TIME: 15 MINUTES

2 tablespoons extra-virgin olive oil, divided

8 ounces extra-firm tofu, drained, cut into ½-inch cubes

3 cups frozen mirepoix

8 cups chicken broth

¼ cup soy sauce

2 packages instant ramen noodles (discard the seasoning packets)

Salt

Freshly ground black pepper

1. In the stockpot over medium heat, heat 1 tablespoon of olive oil. Add the tofu and cook until crispy and brown, about 5 minutes. Set aside.

2. In the same pot over medium heat, heat the remaining 1 tablespoon of olive oil. Add the mirepoix and cook for 5 minutes. Add the chicken broth and soy sauce, and bring to a simmer.

3. Add the ramen noodles and simmer until soft, 3 or 4 minutes. Add the cooked tofu and stir. Season with salt and pepper and serve.

INGREDIENT TIP: You can also use medium-firm or soft tofu in this soup. However, you have to handle soft tofu very gently due to its delicate texture. When using either medium-firm or soft tofu, skip the stir-frying in step 1 and follow the rest of the recipe.

PER SERVING Calories: 402; Total Fat: 20g; Saturated Fat: 6g; Cholesterol: 0mg; Sodium: 2,110mg; Total Carbohydrates: 30g; Sugars: 3g; Protein: 22g

Mushroom Udon Soup

DAIRY-FREE • NUT-FREE • VEGAN

Udon noodles are thick and chewy, and they're delicious served in hot broth. This one is flavored with ginger, soy sauce, and mushrooms. Feel free to add more vegetables as well as any tofu or leftover meat you have on hand.

SERVES 4
PREP TIME: 10 MINUTES
COOK TIME: 15 MINUTES

2 tablespoons extra-virgin olive oil

1 tablespoon minced fresh ginger

1 cup sliced white mushrooms

8 cups vegetable broth

¼ cup soy sauce

2 (7.1-ounce) packages fresh udon noodles

Salt

Freshly ground black pepper

Optional garnish:

2 scallions, thinly sliced

1. In the stockpot over medium heat, heat the olive oil. Add the ginger and mushrooms and cook until fragrant, about 1 minute.

2. Add the broth and soy sauce, bring to a boil, and cook for 5 minutes. Add the udon, reduce the heat, and cook for another 5 minutes. Season with salt and pepper.

3. Distribute the soup evenly among bowls, garnish with scallions, if using, and serve.

INGREDIENT TIP: Udon are thick wheat flour noodles commonly used in Japanese cooking. You can substitute fresh pasta noodles or fresh or dried whole-wheat spaghetti. Adjust the noodle cooking time according to the package if you make a change.

PER SERVING Calories: 334; Total Fat: 11g; Saturated Fat: 2g; Cholesterol: 0mg; Sodium: 2,741mg; Total Carbohydrates: 43g; Sugars: 2g; Protein: 11g

Hong Kong Breakfast Macaroni Soup

STOCKPOT

DAIRY-FREE · NUT-FREE

Macaroni soup is a staple breakfast item in Hong Kong. You can find it just about any-where, from neighborhood diners to fast-food restaurants. It's usually served with a fried egg on top and deli ham (or Spam!). Feel free to experiment with any meats or vegetables you happen to have.

SERVES 4
PREP TIME: 10 MINUTES
COOK TIME: 30 MINUTES

2 cups dried elbow macaroni

Salt

4 tablespoons extra-virgin olive oil, divided

4 eggs

6 cups chicken broth

1 cup frozen mixed peas and carrots

1 teaspoon soy sauce

Freshly ground black pepper

Optional garnish:

Sesame oil

1. Bring a stockpot of water to a boil. Season with salt and cook the macaroni for 8 to 10 minutes, or according to the package instructions. Drain and set aside.

2. In the same pot over medium heat, heat 1 tablespoon of olive oil. Crack 1 egg into the pot and fry it sunny-side up by cooking until the top of the white is set but the yolk is still runny, 2 to 3 minutes. Set aside. Repeat with the remaining 3 tablespoons of oil and remaining 3 eggs, turning the heat down if the oil begins to pop.

3. Add the broth and the peas and carrots to the pot, and bring to a boil. Add the cooked macaroni and the soy sauce, and season with salt and pepper.

4. Ladle the soup into bowls. Top each with a fried egg and drizzle with sesame oil, if using, and serve.

VARIATION: For extra protein, add cooked shredded chicken to this soup.

PER SERVING Calories: 412; Total Fat: 21g; Saturated Fat: 4g; Cholesterol: 162mg; Sodium: 1,338mg; Total Carbohydrates: 35g; Sugars: 4g; Protein: 19g

 # Tortellini Soup

NUT-FREE · VEGETARIAN

I love this dish because it can be made entirely with pantry items. On its own, the tortellini might seem like a lackluster dinner, but simmered in a rich tomato broth flavored with garlic and onions, it becomes a proper—not to mention delicious—meal.

SERVES 4
PREP TIME: 10 MINUTES
COOK TIME: 25 MINUTES

2 tablespoons extra-virgin olive oil

4 garlic cloves, mashed

1 onion, diced

1 (15-ounce) can whole plum tomatoes

4 cups vegetable broth

1 (19-ounce) package frozen cheese tortellini

Salt

Freshly ground black pepper

1. In the stockpot over medium heat, heat the olive oil. Add the garlic and onion and cook for 5 minutes.

2. Crush the tomatoes by gently squeezing them with your hands. Add them with their juices and the vegetable broth, and bring to a simmer.

3. Add the tortellini to the pot and cook according to the package instructions. Season with salt and pepper and serve.

PREP TIP: Mashing the garlic releases more flavor and makes this soup more delicious. A mortar and pestle is great for this, but if you don't have one, you can use a chef's knife. Place the peeled garlic clove on a cutting board. Lay the side of the blade on the garlic clove and press down with the heel of your palm to smash it. Sprinkle with salt and chop coarsely until the garlic turns into a smooth paste.

PER SERVING Calories: 413; Total Fat: 14g; Saturated Fat: 5g; Cholesterol: 40mg; Sodium: 1,176mg; Total Carbohydrates: 54g; Sugars: 9g; Protein: 18g

Quick and Easy French Onion Soup

NUT-FREE

I think of French onion soup as a cook-all-day kind of dish, but this recipe proves it can be on the table quick—and still be satisfying and flavorful. The trick is to sauté the onions well before adding a rich beef broth. If you want to make it extra special, ladle the soup into oven-safe ramekins. Top each bowl with a slice of bread and a layer of cheese and run it under the broiler for a few minutes, until the cheese is melted and golden brown.

SERVES 4
PREP TIME: 5 MINUTES
COOK TIME: 30 MINUTES

2 tablespoons extra-virgin olive oil

4 cups sliced onions

2 (14-ounce) cans beef broth

1 teaspoon dried thyme

Salt

1 cup shredded Swiss cheese

4 French bread slices, toasted

1. In the stockpot over medium heat, heat the olive oil. Add the onion and cook until tender and golden brown, about 10 minutes. Add the beef broth and thyme and let simmer for 20 minutes. Season with salt.

2. Ladle the hot soup into bowls, top with the cheese, and serve with the French bread.

COOK IT SLOW: You can also make this soup in a slow cooker. Combine everything in step 1 and cook on low for 3 hours. Then finish the soup as in step 2.

PER SERVING Calories: 322 Total Fat: 15g; Saturated Fat: 6g; Cholesterol: 25mg; Sodium: 873mg; Total Carbohydrates: 31g; Sugars: 6g; Protein: 16g

Corn Chowder

STOCKPOT • SLOW COOKER

GLUTEN-FREE • NUT-FREE • VEGETARIAN

Corn to me represents the height of fresh, sweet summer produce, but it holds up to freezing surprisingly well. With frozen corn kernels, you can have that bright, sunshiney flavor any time of the year. This thick, potato-studded soup is perfect on a cold winter night.

SERVES 4
PREP TIME: 10 MINUTES
COOK TIME: 20 MINUTES

2 tablespoons extra-virgin olive oil

1 medium onion, chopped

4 cups frozen corn, thawed

2 small russet potatoes, peeled and diced

2 cups vegetable broth

1 cup milk

Salt

Freshly ground black pepper

1. In the stockpot over medium heat, heat the olive oil. Add the onion and cook for 5 minutes.

2. Add the corn, potatoes, broth, and milk and bring to a simmer. Cook for 15 minutes.

3. Transfer 2 cups of the soup to a blender and purée until completely smooth. Return the puréed soup to the pot. Mix well, season with salt and pepper, and serve.

COOK IT SLOW: You can also make this soup in a slow cooker. Combine the olive oil, onion, corn, potatoes, broth, and milk, and cook on low for 4 hours. Then finish the soup as in step 3.

PER SERVING Calories: 246; Total Fat: 10g; Saturated Fat: 2g; Cholesterol: 5mg; Sodium: 456mg; Total Carbohydrates: 35g; Sugars: 8g; Protein: 8g

Sweet Potato Thai Curry Soup

STOCKPOT • SLOW COOKER

DAIRY-FREE • GLUTEN-FREE • NUT-FREE

Thai curry paste is a great condiment to keep in your pantry or refrigerator. Just a spoonful adds layers of flavor—sweet, salty, tangy, spicy—to a dish. Combined with coconut milk, it makes a rich broth for this soup that's fortified with sweet potatoes, chicken, and broccoli.

SERVES 4
PREP TIME: 15 MINUTES
COOK TIME: 30 MINUTES

2 tablespoons extra-virgin olive oil

2 tablespoons Thai red curry paste or Massaman curry paste

2 cups peeled, diced sweet potatoes

8 ounces boneless, skinless chicken breast, cut into small pieces

2 small broccoli heads, florets separated and stems chopped

1 (14-ounce) can coconut milk

2 cups water

Optional garnish:

1 cup fresh cilantro

1. In the stockpot over medium-high heat, heat the olive oil until hot. Add the curry paste and cook for 1 minute, stirring. Add the sweet potatoes, chicken, and broccoli and cook for 8 minutes.

2. Add the coconut milk and water to the pot, and whisk until combined. Bring just to a boil, then reduce the heat, cover, and simmer gently for about 20 minutes, stirring occasionally.

3. Ladle the soup into bowls. Garnish with the cilantro, if using, and serve.

COOK IT SLOW: You can also make this soup in a slow cooker. Combine all the ingredients except the cilantro in a slow cooker and cook on high for 3 hours. Then finish the soup as in step 3.

PER SERVING Calories: 438; Total Fat: 34g; Saturated Fat: 22g; Cholesterol: 36mg; Sodium: 470mg; Total Carbohydrates: 20g; Sugars: 6g; Protein: 15g

Broccoli and Cheese Soup

STOCKPOT • SLOW COOKER

EXTRA-QUICK • GLUTEN-FREE • NUT-FREE

I love broccoli and cheese soup because it's both naughty and nice at the same time—it's loaded with super nutritious broccoli, then thickened with sinfully rich and flavorful cheese and heavy cream. It's an obvious choice on a cold night, but I could eat this any time.

SERVES 4
PREP TIME: 5 MINUTES
COOK TIME: 15 MINUTES

1 tablespoon extra-virgin olive oil

3 garlic cloves, minced

4 cups broccoli florets

4 cups chicken broth

1 cup heavy (whipping) cream

Salt

Freshly ground black pepper

2 cups shredded cheddar cheese

1. In the stockpot over medium heat, heat the olive oil. Sauté the garlic for 1 minute.

2. Add the broccoli and chicken broth. Bring to a simmer over high heat, then cook for 10 minutes, or until the broccoli is barely tender and still bright green.

3. Stir in the heavy cream and cook for 2 to 3 minutes. Season with salt and pepper. Remove the pot from the heat and allow to cool for 1 to 2 minutes. Add the cheese, stirring constantly until it is melted, and serve.

COOK IT SLOW: You can also make this soup in a slow cooker. Simply add the garlic, broccoli, and chicken broth to the slow cooker, and cook on low for 3 hours. Then finish the soup right in the cooker, as described in step 3.

PER SERVING Calories: 536; Total Fat: 46g; Saturated Fat: 26g; Cholesterol: 141mg; Sodium: 1,206mg; Total Carbohydrates: 10g; Sugars: 3g; Protein: 23g

 # Salmon Bisque

EXTRA-QUICK · GLUTEN-FREE · NUT-FREE

Salmon bisque does not have to cost you an arm and a leg. And using canned salmon means you don't have to worry about finding fresh salmon if you are making this meal last minute. This is an excellent recipe for when the weather gets colder or you need something warm and comforting in 20 minutes.

SERVES 4 to 6
PREP TIME: 5 MINUTES
COOK TIME: 15 MINUTES

4 cups chicken broth

2 cups cauliflower florets

2 bay leaves

2 cups milk

2 (5-ounce) cans pink salmon, drained

Salt

Freshly ground black pepper

1. In the stockpot over high heat, combine the broth, cauliflower, and bay leaves. Bring to a boil and cook for 10 minutes.

2. Lower the heat, and stir in the milk and salmon. Simmer for 5 minutes, season with salt and pepper, and serve.

PREP TIP: Cutting cauliflower into florets is so easy. Quarter the cauliflower and remove the stem. It will naturally fall apart into large florets, then cut them into smaller florets. Wash the cauliflower right after cutting it, so you can rinse out all the nooks and crannies.

PER SERVING Calories: 206; Total Fat: 8g; Saturated Fat: 3g; Cholesterol: 41mg; Sodium: 906mg; Total Carbohydrates: 10g; Sugars: 7g; Protein: 24g

 # Crab Bisque

GLUTEN-FREE • NUT-FREE

A velvety and creamy crab bisque is the perfect comfort food in the winter. And it is so easy to make. The seductive mix of shallot, cream, chicken broth, and crab will make this a quick favorite. Substitute another seafood, like frozen shrimp or canned lobster, for a change of pace.

SERVES 4
PREP TIME: 10 MINUTES
COOK TIME: 20 MINUTES

4 tablespoons extra-virgin olive oil

1 shallot, finely chopped

1 cup frozen mirepoix

2 cups chicken broth

1 (6-ounce) can crabmeat, drained, flaked, any cartilage removed

2 cups heavy (whipping) cream

Salt

Freshly ground black pepper

1. In the stockpot over medium heat, heat the olive oil. Add the shallot and mirepoix and cook for 5 minutes.

2. Add the chicken broth and cook for another 3 minutes. Transfer to a food processor or blender (or use an immersion blender) and blend until completely puréed.

3. Return the puréed soup to the pot. Add the crabmeat and cook over low heat for 5 minutes. Stir in the heavy cream and simmer for 5 minutes, or until just thickened. Season with salt and pepper and serve.

COOK IT SLOW: You can also make this soup in a slow cooker. Add the shallot, mirepoix, and broth to the slow cooker and cook on low for 3 hours. Then purée the soup and finish as in step 3.

PER SERVING Calories: 622; Total Fat: 59g; Saturated Fat: 30g; Cholesterol: 186mg; Sodium: 835mg; Total Carbohydrates: 10g; Sugars: 2g; Protein: 14g

Soba Noodle Salad

STOCKPOT

EXTRA-QUICK · DAIRY-FREE · NUT-FREE · VEGAN

Soba noodles are thin Japanese buckwheat noodles. They cook quickly and are delicious eaten either hot or cold. This soba noodle salad is a light, flavorful dinner. It gets a protein boost from shelled edamame. Edamame (boiled green soy beans) are available out of the pod (shelled) or in the pod (unshelled). To enjoy unshelled edamame, add them to a pot of boiling, salted water. Boil frozen edamame for 1 to 2 minutes or 5 to 6 minutes for fresh edamame. Drain and rinse with cold water. Enjoy this healthy vegan option on a warm summer night.

SERVES 4
PREP TIME: 10 MINUTES
COOK TIME: 10 MINUTES

6 ounces dried soba noodles or thin whole-wheat spaghetti

1½ cups frozen shelled edamame or frozen peas, thawed

1 tablespoon soy sauce

½ cup seasoned rice vinegar

1 tablespoon sesame oil

Optional garnish:

1 cup cucumber matchstick pieces

2 scallions, thinly sliced

1. Fill the stockpot with water and bring to a boil over high heat. Add the soba noodles and edamame, and cook for 3 minutes. Drain.

2. In a large mixing bowl, mix the soy sauce, rice vinegar, and sesame oil. Add the noodle mixture. Garnish with cucumber and scallions, if using, and serve.

VARIATION: In the summertime, this dish is best eaten cold. To enjoy it cold, mix up everything as instructed, but leave off the scallions. Refrigerate the salad for 20 to 30 minutes. Garnish with the scallions when you are ready to eat.

PER SERVING Calories: 230; Total Fat: 4g; Saturated Fat: 1g; Cholesterol: 0mg; Sodium: 687mg; Total Carbohydrates: 42g; Sugars: 5g; Protein: 10g

Japanese Curry with Udon

STOCKPOT · SLOW COOKER

DAIRY-FREE · NUT-FREE · VEGAN

This is a meat-free take on this famous Japanese curry. Rich and comforting flavors take your taste buds straight to the streets of Tokyo. One of the most popular dishes in Japan, Japanese curry is commonly served over rice, with udon, or with bread.

SERVES 4
PREP TIME: 10 MINUTES
COOK TIME: 20 MINUTES

2 tablespoons extra-virgin olive oil

1 medium onion, diced

1 cup diced carrot

7 cups water

5 ounces Japanese curry mix (also called Vermont curry or golden curry)

5 ounces (about 4 cups) baby spinach

2 (200-gram/7-ounce) packages udon or 14 ounces dried whole-wheat spaghetti

1. In the stockpot over medium-high heat, heat the olive oil. Add the onion and cook for 2 minutes. Add the carrot and water to the pot, and reduce the heat to low.

2. Add the curry mix and stir well, so the pieces of the curry mix dissolve, and cook for 15 minutes.

3. Add the spinach and udon. Cook for another 3 minutes and serve.

COOK IT SLOW: You can make this curry in a slow cooker. Add all the ingredients except the udon and cook on low heat for 4 hours. Add the udon and cook for another 15 to 20 minutes. Serve right away.

PER SERVING Calories: 465; Total Fat: 10g; Saturated Fat: 2g; Cholesterol: 0mg; Sodium: 261mg; Total Carbohydrates: 82g; Sugars: 3g; Protein: 16g

Cherry Tomato Pasta

NUT-FREE · VEGETARIAN

This is a fresh, bright pasta dish that I love to make in the summer when cherry tomatoes are at their peak. The chopped fresh basil and minced garlic really bring it to life. I have to be careful when I make this one because I won't stop eating until the bowl is empty.

SERVES 4
PREP TIME: 10 MINUTES
COOK TIME: 20 MINUTES

Salt

8 ounces (about 4 cups) any shape dried pasta

3 tablespoons extra-virgin olive oil

2 garlic cloves, finely chopped

2 pints cherry tomatoes

Freshly ground black pepper

1 cup finely chopped fresh basil

¼ cup grated Parmesan cheese

1. Fill the stockpot with water and bring to a boil, and season with salt. Add the pasta and cook according to the package directions or until al dente (firm to the bite). Drain and transfer to a large bowl.

2. In the same pot over medium-high heat, heat the olive oil. Add the garlic and cherry tomatoes. Season with salt and pepper, and cook for 5 minutes. Add the basil and cook for another 2 minutes, or until the tomatoes burst and release their juices to form a sauce.

3. Toss the pasta with the tomato sauce, sprinkle on the Parmesan cheese, and serve.

INGREDIENT TIP: Although you can store fresh basil in the refrigerator, it is better to store it at room temperature. To keep it fresh, place the stems in a glass jar of water, cover loosely in a thin and light plastic bag, and leave it on the countertop.

PER SERVING Calories: 359; Total Fat: 13g; Saturated Fat: 3g; Cholesterol: 5mg; Sodium: 78mg; Total Carbohydrates: 50g; Sugars: 6g; Protein: 12g

Spaghetti with Pistachio Pesto

SAUCEPAN

EXTRA-QUICK · FREEZER-FRIENDLY · VEGETARIAN

Pistachios are both easier to find and less expensive than the more traditional pine nuts. Plus, I love the rich, almost fruity flavor of pistachios. Lots of fresh basil, garlic, and Parmesan cheese make this into an irresistible pesto sauce that's perfect on pasta. Make a double batch of this sauce and use the leftovers as a sandwich spread or as a sauce for pizza.

SERVES 4
PREP TIME: 10 MINUTES
COOK TIME: 10 MINUTES

Salt

1½ cups shelled, dry-roasted, salted pistachios

1 cup grated Parmesan cheese, plus more for garnish

½ cup fresh basil leaves

3 garlic cloves

Freshly ground black pepper

½ cup extra-virgin olive oil

10 ounces fresh spaghetti

1. Fill the saucepan with water and salt generously. Bring to a boil.

2. While waiting for the water to boil, add the pistachios, Parmesan cheese, basil, and garlic to a food processor, and season with salt and pepper. Pulse to combine. While the machine is running, stream in the olive oil through the spout. Blend until creamy and fully combined. Adjust the seasonings as needed.

3. Add the pasta to the boiling water and cook for 4 minutes, or until al dente (firm to the bite). Drain and transfer to a large mixing bowl.

4. Add the pesto to the cooked pasta, and toss to coat. Add a little more olive oil or pasta water if the pesto needs more liquid. Serve warm with more Parmesan cheese on top.

FROM THE FREEZER: Fresh pesto can be stored in an airtight jar for up to 1 week in the refrigerator, or 9 to 12 months frozen. Freeze in an ice cube tray, then pop the cubes into a zip-top bag.

PER SERVING Calories: 578; Total Fat: 38g; Saturated Fat: 8g; Cholesterol: 72mg; Sodium: 339mg; Total Carbohydrates: 44g; Sugars: 1g; Protein: 20g

Spaghetti alle Vongole

SAUCEPAN

DAIRY-FREE · NUT-FREE

Spaghetti with clams is a classic Italian dish that's surprisingly easy to make. To make this recipe even easier, you can use canned clams or frozen shrimp. A little bread, a little wine, and some candlelight make this a great date-night meal.

SERVES 4
PREP TIME: 10 MINUTES
COOK TIME: 15 MINUTES

Salt

10 ounces fresh spaghetti

½ pound littleneck clams

¼ cup extra-virgin olive oil

3 garlic cloves, finely chopped

1 teaspoon red pepper flakes

Freshly ground black pepper

⅓ cup chopped fresh parsley

1. Fill the saucepan with water and salt generously. Bring to a boil. Add the pasta and cook according to the package directions or until al dente (firm to the bite). Reserve 2 cups of the pasta water, then drain the pasta and set aside.

2. Wash the clams thoroughly under cold running water to get rid of all the sand in the shells. Return the pot to the stove. Over medium heat, add the olive oil. Add the garlic and red pepper flakes and sauté for 30 seconds. Add the clams, then turn to high heat. Cover and cook for 5 minutes, until all the clams have opened.

3. Add the pasta back to the pot. Add some of the pasta water, if it needs liquid. Stir over gentle heat for 2 minutes. Season with salt and pepper.

4. Transfer to a serving platter, garnish with the parsley, and serve.

PREP TIP: To clean the clams, soak in fresh water for 20 minutes, then pull the clams out of the water with your hands. Do not pour through a strainer, as the sand will remain stuck in the clams. Then use a firm, soft brush to remove any dirt. If you find any opened clams before cooking, discard them.

PER SERVING Calories: 359; Total Fat: 15g; Saturated Fat: 2g; Cholesterol: 71mg; Sodium: 53mg; Total Carbohydrates: 51g; Sugars: 0g; Protein: 16g

Cheese Ravioli with Mushroom Sauce

STOCKPOT

NUT-FREE • VEGETARIAN

When sautéed with shallot and fresh herbs, mushrooms take on an almost meaty quality, and they form the base of a sauce that pairs well with the rich cheese ravioli filling. This is one of my all-time favorite vegetarian pasta dishes.

SERVES 4 to 6
PREP TIME: 10 MINUTES
COOK TIME: 15 MINUTES

Salt

1 (20-ounce) package fresh cheese ravioli

2 tablespoons extra-virgin olive oil

1 large shallot, thinly sliced

2 fresh rosemary sprigs or 1 teaspoon dried rosemary

2 cups sliced cremini mushrooms

Freshly ground black pepper

½ cup grated Parmesan cheese, plus more for garnish

1. Fill the stockpot with water and salt generously. Bring to a boil. Add the ravioli and cook for 5 minutes, or 1 minute less than the package directions. Reserve 1 cup of the pasta water, drain the ravioli, and set aside.

2. In the same pot over medium-high heat, heat the olive oil. Add the shallot, rosemary, and mushrooms. Season with salt and pepper and cook for 5 minutes.

3. Add the pasta to the pot with ⅓ cup of the reserved pasta water. Add the Parmesan cheese, and toss the pasta until the sauce is creamy. Add more pasta water, if needed. Garnish with more Parmesan cheese and serve.

INGREDIENT TIP: You can store dried rosemary in a glass container or in bottles of extra-virgin olive oil. Use 2 table-spoons of this rosemary oil when making this recipe again.

PER SERVING Calories: 513; Total Fat: 19g; Saturated Fat: 3g; Cholesterol: 60mg; Sodium: 898mg; Total Carbohydrates: 63g; Sugars: 1g; Protein: 24g

 # Italian Sausage Pasta

SAUCEPAN

DAIRY-FREE · NUT-FREE

This dish is super simple to make and has a delicious thick sauce. The savory garlic flavor from the marinara sauce creates a full flavor. You can use any type of pasta with this. Just remember that thin angel-hair pasta cooks very quickly. A thicker pasta will need more time to cook.

SERVES 4 to 6
PREP TIME: 5 MINUTES
COOK TIME: 25 MINUTES

Salt

1 pound dried
angel-hair pasta

2 tablespoons extra-virgin
olive oil

1½ pounds bulk Italian
pork sausage

1 (24-ounce) jar
marinara sauce

1 bunch basil leaves, torn, plus
more for garnish

1 tablespoon grated
Parmesan cheese

1. Fill the saucepan with water and salt generously. Bring to a boil. Drop in the angel-hair pasta and cook for 4 to 5 minutes, or until al dente (firm to the bite). Drain and set aside.

2. Return the pot to the stove over medium heat, add the olive oil, and heat for 30 seconds. Add the sausage. Cook, breaking up the meat as it cooks, for 10 minutes, or until no more pink is visible.

3. Add the marinara sauce and basil to the pot and cook for 3 minutes more.

4. To serve, divide the pasta among bowls and top with the meat sauce. Sprinkle with the Parmesan cheese, garnish with more basil, and serve.

INGREDIENT TIP: Bulk sausage is sausage meat without the casing. If you can't find it, just slit the casings on regular sausages and use a spoon to scrape out the meat.

PER SERVING Calories: 940; Total Fat: 65g; Saturated Fat: 21g; Cholesterol: 130mg; Sodium: 1,856mg; Total Carbohydrates: 53g; Sugars: 7g; Protein: 34g

Beef Stroganoff

STOCKPOT

NUT-FREE

Beef stroganoff is a bit of a throwback dish, but it's easy to see why it has never really fallen out of favor. Strips of flavorful top sirloin are pan sautéed and then tossed with beef broth and sour cream to make a meaty sauce that is delicious served over egg noodles or any pasta you happen to have on hand.

SERVES 4
PREP TIME: 5 MINUTES
COOK TIME: 25 MINUTES

Salt

8 ounces dried medium egg noodles

1 tablespoon extra-virgin olive oil

1 pound top sirloin steak, cut into strips

Freshly ground black pepper

1¾ cups beef broth

½ cup sour cream

2 tablespoons minced fresh parsley

1. Fill the stockpot with water and salt generously. Bring to a boil. Cook the egg noodles, stirring occasionally, according to the package instructions. Drain and set aside.

2. In the same pot over high heat, heat the olive oil. Add the beef strips, season with salt and pepper, and cook for 5 minutes, or until the beef turns brown. Move the beef to one side of the pot.

3. Add the broth and sour cream, and whisk well. Keep whisking until no clumps remain. Return the meat to the pot and continue stirring over low heat for 10 minutes.

4. To serve, divide the noodles among four bowls and top with the beef and sauce. Garnish with the parsley and serve.

VARIATION: You can use your favorite pasta, such as linguine, instead of egg noodles.

PER SERVING Calories: 438; Total Fat: 16g; Saturated Fat: 7g; Cholesterol: 89mg; Sodium: 548mg; Total Carbohydrates: 37g; Sugars: 1g; Protein: 34g

Dutch Oven

If you don't have a Dutch oven, trust me, you need one. A good Dutch oven can be the most important—and versatile—cooking vessel in your kitchen. Dutch ovens are great for both stove top and oven use, and they can act as a kind of oven slow cooker. They are ideal for braising meat; cooking soups, stews, and sauces; boiling water for pasta; frying chicken; and even baking bread.

Dutch ovens have thick walls and a tight-fitting lid. They are usually made of cast iron coated with enamel, but you can also find cast aluminum and ceramic ones. They range in size from 2 quarts to 16 quarts, and some have even larger capacities. I recommend buying an enameled cast-iron Dutch oven. They are expensive, but they can be used for any ingredients, including acidic foods. A midsize, 5.5-quart one is perfect for the recipes in this book.

For all their good qualities, Dutch ovens are heavy and cumbersome, which can intimidate inexperienced chefs. So here are some helpful guidelines for using your Dutch oven.

Italian Sausage Jambalaya, page 70

- Because Dutch ovens are great at retaining heat, cooking on the stove top over medium-high or high heat is just too hot. Cooking at **medium heat** is more than sufficient for this pot.

- You should **never preheat a Dutch oven while empty,** as this can cause the enamel to crack, so drizzle olive oil in first and then switch the stove top on. Never put a cold, empty pot in a hot oven to heat up, either. Instead, put it into a cold oven and let the two slowly preheat together.

- Play it safe and **use utensils made from silicone, wood, or heat-resistant plastic** that won't run any risk of scratching the precious enamel coating.

- While Dutch ovens can technically go into the dishwasher, doing so can dull the enamel coating, so **hand washing** your pot is best. When you do so, make sure you **dry it completely**, as any excess moisture can cause rust to form.

Lasagna Soup

DAIRY-FREE · NUT-FREE · VEGETARIAN

Who doesn't love lasagna? The only problem is that it is labor-intensive to prepare, and on top of that, it also needs to cook for up to an hour. This soup is a clever way around that conundrum. Put the classic lasagna ingredients into a Dutch oven and simmer until the pasta is tender and the flavors meld. Top it with cheese and voilà! Lasagna in a bowl.

SERVES 6 to 8
PREP TIME: 5 MINUTES
COOK TIME: 20 MINUTES

2 tablespoons extra-virgin olive oil

1 small onion, diced

2 cups frozen mirepoix

1 cup jarred marinara sauce

4 cups vegetable broth

Salt

Freshly ground black pepper

8 sheets dried lasagna noodles, broken into about-2-inch squares

Optional garnish:

½ cup shredded Parmesan cheese

1. In a Dutch oven over medium heat, heat the olive oil. Add the onion and mirepoix and cook for 3 to 5 minutes.

2. Stir in the marinara sauce and broth, and season with salt and pepper. Bring to a boil. Stir in the broken lasagna and return to a boil. Simmer uncovered for 10 to 15 minutes, or until the pasta is tender.

3. Sprinkle the cheese on top, if using, and serve.

VARIATION: If you want more protein in this dish, you can add 1 pound of lean ground beef. Add it right after the vegetables in step 1, and give it a few minutes to brown before you move on to step 2.

PER SERVING Calories: 614; Total Fat: 9g; Saturated Fat: 1g; Cholesterol: 40mg; Sodium: 656mg; Total Carbohydrates: 114g; Sugars: 8g; Protein: 20g

Gnocchi Soup

EXTRA-QUICK · NUT-FREE

Potato-based gnocchi make a nice change from the usual noodles in this soup. Add a flavorful spiced Spanish chorizo sausage and fresh spinach, and you've got yourself a perfect snuggle-on-the-sofa movie-night meal.

SERVES 4
PREP TIME: 5 MINUTES
COOK TIME: 10 MINUTES

1 tablespoon extra-virgin olive oil

1½ cups Spanish chorizo sausage, diced

6 cups reduced-sodium chicken broth

1 (16-ounce) package frozen mini potato gnocchi

1 (6-ounce) package baby spinach

1 cup milk

Salt

Freshly ground black pepper

1. In the Dutch oven over medium heat, heat the olive oil. Add the chorizo sausage and cook for 5 minutes.

2. Add the chicken broth and bring to a simmer. Add the gnocchi and continue to simmer until the gnocchi is al dente (firm to the bite), about 3 minutes.

3. Add the spinach and milk, and cook until the spinach is wilted, about 2 minutes more. Season with salt and pepper and serve.

INGREDIENT TIP: Spanish chorizo is not the same as Mexican chorizo. Spanish chorizo is a cured pork sausage, and Mexican chorizo is made with fresh minced pork.

PER SERVING Calories: 415; Total Fat: 12g; Saturated Fat: 4g; Cholesterol: 50mg; Sodium: 2,023mg; Total Carbohydrates: 49g; Sugars: 4g; Protein: 27g

Spicy Sausage and Kale Soup

GLUTEN-FREE • NUT-FREE

If you're looking for a warm winter soup that is packed full of protein and iron, it does not get any better than this. The spicy flavor of the sausage mixed with the savory broth, fresh kale, and creamy, rich half-and-half make this a guaranteed family favorite.

SERVES 4
PREP TIME: 10 MINUTES
COOK TIME: 30 MINUTES

1 pound spicy Italian sausage

2 cups torn kale leaves

6 cups chicken broth

2 russet potatoes, peeled and cubed

1 cup half-and-half

Salt

Freshly ground black pepper

Optional garnish:

1 teaspoon red pepper flakes

1. Remove the casings from the sausage and discard, then crumble the meat. Discard the stems from the kale, and coarsely chop the leaves into bite-size pieces.

2. In the Dutch oven over medium heat, cook the sausage for 5 minutes. Add the chicken broth and potatoes. Bring to a boil, then let simmer for 15 minutes.

3. Add the kale and half-and-half. Cook, covered, for 10 minutes. Season with salt and pepper.

4. Garnish with the red pepper flakes, if using, and serve.

COOK IT SLOW: You can also make this soup in a slow cooker. Remove the casing from the sausage and discard, then crumble the meat. In a slow cooker, combine the meat, coarsely chopped kale, chicken broth, and potatoes. Cook on high for 4 hours. Add the half-and-half and cook for another 10 minutes. Season with salt and pepper, then garnish with the red pepper flakes, if using.

PER SERVING Calories: 617; Total Fat: 45g; Saturated Fat: 18g; Cholesterol: 108mg; Sodium: 2,055mg; Total Carbohydrates: 25g; Sugars: 2g; Protein: 28g

Mushroom Risotto

GLUTEN-FREE · NUT-FREE · VEGETARIAN

Risotto has a reputation for being difficult to make, but this recipe proves that it's almost as easy as making pasta. Mushrooms add a meaty bite and intense earthy flavor to this quick vegetarian meal.

SERVES 4
PREP TIME: 10 MINUTES
COOK TIME: 20 MINUTES

3 tablespoons extra-virgin olive oil, divided

1 pound mushrooms (preferably chanterelles or stemmed shiitakes), quartered

2 shallots, thinly sliced

1¼ cups arborio rice

3¼ cups vegetable broth, divided

Salt

Freshly ground black pepper

1 cup grated Parmesan cheese

Optional garnish:

Thinly sliced fresh chives

1. In the Dutch oven, combine 1 tablespoon of olive oil and the mushrooms. Cook for 7 to 9 minutes over medium heat, stirring, until softened. Remove the mushrooms and set aside.

2. Add the remaining 2 tablespoons of olive oil and the shallots to the pot over medium-high heat, and sauté until translucent, about 3 minutes.

3. Add the rice and cook for 1 minute, stirring constantly. Add about half of the broth and cook for 5 minutes, simmering over medium-low heat, until the liquid is nearly absorbed. Taste and season with salt. Continue stirring until the rice is just tender and the mixture is creamy. Add the remaining broth and stir often, until the rice absorbs the broth. Season with salt and pepper.

4. When the rice is tender but still chewy, add the Parmesan cheese and cooked mushrooms, and carefully combine into the risotto. Spoon the risotto into warm bowls. Top with chives, if using, and serve.

INGREDIENT TIP: Keep fresh mushrooms in a dark paper bag in the refrigerator.

PER SERVING Calories: 492; Total Fat: 20g; Saturated Fat: 6g; Cholesterol: 26mg; Sodium: 589mg; Total Carbohydrates: 60g; Sugars: 5g; Protein: 22g

 # Red Pepper Risotto

DUTCH OVEN

GLUTEN-FREE · NUT-FREE · VEGETARIAN

This is another easy vegetarian risotto dish that I love to make in the summer when red bell peppers are all over the farmers' market. The bright red color makes it as good to look at as it is to eat. Creamy and tangy goat cheese goes well with the summer flavors here.

SERVES 4
PREP TIME: 10 MINUTES
COOK TIME: 30 MINUTES

2 tablespoons extra-virgin olive oil

1 small onion, finely chopped

3 red bell peppers, seeded and finely chopped

1¼ cups arborio rice

3¼ cups vegetable broth

Salt

1 cup crumbled goat cheese

1. In the Dutch oven over medium heat, heat the olive oil. Add the onion and bell peppers, and cook for 2 to 3 minutes, stirring until softened.

2. Add the rice and cook for 1 minute, stirring constantly. Add about half of the broth and cook for 5 minutes, until the liquid is nearly absorbed. Taste and add salt if needed.

3. Add the remaining broth. Continue stirring until the rice absorbs all the broth and is just tender to the bite, 15 to 20 minutes.

4. Spoon the risotto into warm bowls, top with the goat cheese, and serve.

INGREDIENT TIP: For a better result, heat your broth before you add it to the rice. That way, the rice will cook evenly. If you use cold both, the rice will cook from the outside in, so you will get fluffy rice that is still hard in the middle.

PER SERVING Calories: 375; Total Fat: 10g; Saturated Fat: 2g; Cholesterol: 5mg; Sodium: 791mg; Total Carbohydrates: 59g; Sugars: 1g; Protein: 11g

Tomato Risotto with Pancetta

DUTCH OVEN

DAIRY-FREE · GLUTEN-FREE · NUT-FREE

This risotto combines juicy tomatoes with salty, meaty pancetta to create a sweet-savory flavor that you will adore. Pancetta is Italian-style bacon, and you can often find it at the deli meat counter of a good supermarket. If you can't find it, thick-cut American-style bacon is a good substitute.

SERVES 3 to 4
PREP TIME: 5 MINUTES
COOK TIME: 30 MINUTES

1 cup diced sweet or spicy pancetta

2 tablespoons extra-virgin olive oil

1¼ cups arborio rice

3¼ cups chicken broth

Salt

¾ cup canned crushed tomatoes

1. In the Dutch oven over medium heat, brown the pancetta until golden brown. Remove from the pan and set aside.

2. Add the oil to the pan and warm for a moment. Then add the rice and cook for 1 minute, stirring constantly. Add about half of the chicken broth. Cook for 5 minutes, until the liquid is nearly absorbed. Taste and add salt if needed.

3. Add the tomatoes and the remaining broth and continue stirring, until the rice absorbs all the broth.

4. Spoon the risotto into warm bowls, top with the cooked pancetta, and serve.

VARIATION: Upgrade this risotto and swap 1 to 2 cups of cooked crab meat for the pancetta. To cook with crab, skip step 1 and add the crab along with the tomatoes in step 3.

PER SERVING Calories: 483; Total Fat: 15g; Saturated Fat: 3g; Cholesterol: 15mg; Sodium: 1,219mg; Total Carbohydrates: 69g; Sugars: 4g; Protein: 15g

Baked Tortellini with Sausage

DUTCH OVEN

NUT-FREE

Layers of cheese-filled pasta, cheese, and sausage finished with a crunchy breadcrumb topping make this a crowd favorite—and it's a great, hearty dish for feeding a crowd, too. This is a dish that really takes advantage of the Dutch oven's stove-top-to-oven versatility.

SERVES 4
PREP TIME: 5 MINUTES
COOK TIME: 25 MINUTES

2 cups water

1 (9-ounce) package dried or fresh cheese tortellini

2 tablespoons extra-virgin olive oil

1 pound Italian sausage, cut into small pieces

1 (15-ounce) jar marinara sauce

Salt

Freshly ground black pepper

1 cup shredded mozzarella cheese

1 cup Italian breadcrumbs

1. Preheat the oven to 375°F.

2. In the Dutch oven, bring the water to a boil. Add the cheese tortellini and cook for about 5 minutes. Drain completely and set aside. In the Dutch oven, heat the olive oil. Add the sausage and cook for 5 minutes, stirring occasionally. Add the cooked tortellini and marinara sauce, and season with salt and pepper. Cook for another 5 minutes, then turn off the heat.

3. Add the mozzarella cheese, stirring occasionally to combine. Sprinkle the breadcrumbs on top, then bake for 10 minutes, or until the top is golden brown. Let it cool a bit, then serve.

INGREDIENT TIP: Whenever possible, buy your Italian sausage from the meat counter. A butcher can offer you better selection and quality and can answer any questions about what goes into the meat mix.

PER SERVING Calories: 655; Total Fat: 30g; Saturated Fat: 8g; Cholesterol: 153mg; Sodium: 1,987mg; Total Carbohydrates: 68g; Sugars: 8g; Protein: 30g

Italian Sausage Jambalaya

DUTCH OVEN

EXTRA-QUICK • DAIRY-FREE • GLUTEN-FREE • NUT-FREE

Jambalaya is a Cajun dish that traditionally combines spicy Southern seasonings with rice, veggies, and various meats, including sausage. This simple version just uses sausage, but you could add a few frozen shrimp or some skinless chicken thighs if you want more variety. For a good precooked, microwavable rice, I like Uncle Ben's and Rice-A-Roni.

SERVES 4
PREP TIME: 5 MINUTES
COOK TIME: 15 MINUTES

3 spicy Italian sausages

2 tablespoons extra-virgin olive oil

2 cups frozen mirepoix

1 cup canned crushed tomatoes

1½ teaspoons Cajun seasoning

2 (8.8-ounce) packages precooked rice

Salt

Freshly ground black pepper

1. Remove the casings from the sausage and discard, then crumble the meat.

2. In the Dutch oven over medium heat, heat the olive oil. Brown the sausage, stirring occasionally, for about 3 minutes. Add the mirepoix and cook until tender, about 4 minutes.

3. Stir in the tomatoes, Cajun seasoning, and rice. Season with salt and pepper. Simmer, stirring occasionally, until slightly thickened, about 5 minutes, and serve.

VARIATION: If you're in the mood for seafood, simply substitute 10 to 15 large shrimp, peeled and deveined, for the sausage. You can also use frozen, but they need to be thawed. Put them in a colander in the sink and run cold water over them for about 5 minutes.

PER SERVING Calories: 504; Total Fat: 24g; Saturated Fat: 7g; Cholesterol: 35mg; Sodium: 1,013mg; Total Carbohydrates: 50g; Sugars: 7g; Protein: 20g

Peppercorn Pork Chops

DUTCH OVEN

DAIRY-FREE · GLUTEN-FREE · NUT-FREE

Black peppercorns are a simple pantry staple that can make a big taste impression. For this recipe they are coarsely crushed rather than ground, so they offer an intense peppery kick as well as add a bit of texture to these meaty chops. A bag of frozen green beans rounds out the meal.

SERVES 4
PREP TIME: 5 MINUTES
COOK TIME: 25 MINUTES

4 (8- to 10-ounce) pork chops, about 1 inch thick, at room temperature

1 tablespoon coarsely crushed black peppercorns

2 tablespoons extra-virgin olive oil

1 (16-ounce) bag frozen French-style green beans

Salt

Freshly ground black pepper

1. Pat the chops dry using a paper towel. Rub each of the pork chops on both sides with the peppercorns, pressing hard.

2. In the Dutch oven over medium heat, heat the olive oil until hot. Add the pork chops and cook, uncovered, for 6 to 8 minutes on each side. Turn off the heat and let them rest in the pot for 5 minutes before transferring them to a plate.

3. Add the green beans to the Dutch oven over medium-high heat and cook until tender, about 5 minutes. Season with salt and pepper, and serve over the pork chops.

INGREDIENT TIP: For a better and juicier result, buy pork chops with bones.

PER SERVING Calories: 315; Total Fat: 15g; Saturated Fat: 4g; Cholesterol: 104mg; Sodium: 109mg; Total Carbohydrates: 8g; Sugars: 2g; Protein: 37g

Chicken Madeira

DUTCH OVEN

GLUTEN-FREE · NUT-FREE

Topping simple chicken breast with asparagus and cheese and coating it in a reduction of beef broth and Madeira wine turn an ordinary chicken into an elevated, restaurant-worthy meal. If you have a little extra time, whip up some mashed potatoes to serve alongside.

SERVES 4
PREP TIME: 10 MINUTES
COOK TIME: 30 MINUTES

4 boneless, skinless chicken breasts

1 tablespoon salt, plus more for seasoning

Freshly ground black pepper

6 cups water

½ pound asparagus, trimmed

2 tablespoons extra-virgin olive oil

2 cups Madeira wine

2 cups beef broth

½ cup shredded mozzarella cheese

Optional garnish:

2 tablespoons chopped fresh parsley

1. Lay the chicken breasts on a cutting board, and cover each with a piece of plastic wrap. Use a mallet or a small, heavy frying pan to pound them to ¼ inch thick. Discard the plastic wrap and lightly season with salt and pepper on both sides of the chicken.

2. Fill the Dutch oven with the water, bring to a boil, and add the salt. Add the asparagus and boil, uncovered, until crisp, tender, and bright green, 2 to 3 minutes. Remove immediately and set aside. Pour out the water.

3. In the Dutch oven over medium heat, heat the olive oil. Cook the chicken for 4 to 5 minutes on each side, until slightly browned and just cooked through. Remove and set aside.

4. Add the Madeira wine and beef broth. Bring to a boil, reduce to a simmer, and cook for 10 to 12 minutes. Return the chicken to the pot, turning it to coat in the sauce.

5. Lay the asparagus and cheese on top of the chicken. Then transfer the Dutch oven to the oven broiler and broil for 3 to 4 minutes, or until the cheese is completely melted. Garnish with the parsley, if using, and serve.

VARIATION: If you don't cook with alcohol, substitute 1 cup of balsamic vinegar for the Madeira wine in step 4. It will add to the complexity of flavors. Let it cook until it is reduced by half, 5 to 8 minutes, then add the chicken and continue with the recipe.

PER SERVING Calories: 407; Total Fat: 10g; Saturated Fat: 2g; Cholesterol: 83mg; Sodium: 547mg; Total Carbohydrates: 15g; Sugars: 3g; Protein: 37g

One-Pot Farfalle Pasta

DUTCH OVEN

NUT-FREE

Baking the pasta directly in the sauce, rather than boiling it first, allows the flavor of the sauce to really permeate it. Combining ground beef with a store-bought tomato sauce gives you a fuss-free pasta sauce that tastes homemade.

SERVES 4
PREP TIME: 5 MINUTES
COOK TIME: 30 MINUTES

2 tablespoons extra-virgin olive oil

1 pound lean ground beef

1 (25-ounce) jar marinara sauce with basil

2 cups water

Salt

Freshly ground black pepper

2 cups dried farfalle (bowtie) pasta

3 cups baby spinach

1½ cups fresh mozzarella cheese, sliced

Optional garnish:

Fresh basil leaves

Grated Parmesan cheese

1. Preheat the oven to 375°F.

2. In the Dutch oven over medium heat, heat the olive oil until hot. Add the ground beef and cook for 8 to 10 minutes, stirring to break the beef into small crumbles. Add the marinara sauce and water. Bring to a boil, stirring occasionally. Season with salt and pepper. Add the pasta and spinach, and mix.

3. Tuck a few slices of fresh mozzarella into the mix, and place the rest on top. Cover and bake for 20 minutes, or until the pasta is tender.

4. Sprinkle fresh basil and Parmesan cheese on top, if using, and serve.

VARIATION: To make this a vegetarian dish, skip the ground beef. Instead, add a pound of diced asparagus or mushrooms—or both.

PER SERVING Calories: 523; Total Fat: 18g; Saturated Fat: 8g; Cholesterol: 100mg; Sodium: 1,222mg; Total Carbohydrates: 48g; Sugars: 10g; Protein: 42g

Sloppy Joe Sandwiches

DUTCH OVEN · SLOW COOKER

DAIRY-FREE · NUT-FREE

Grab extra napkins! This classic sloppy joe recipe is always a winner. Plus, it's super easy to double or triple when you have a crowd to feed. I love that it can be whipped up in the Dutch oven on the stove top or cooked "hands-free" in a slow cooker.

SERVES 8
PREP TIME: 5 MINUTES
COOK TIME: 45 MINUTES

2 tablespoons extra-virgin olive oil

1 small onion, diced

1 pound ground beef

1 cup jarred tomato sauce

2 tablespoons Worcestershire sauce

Salt

Freshly ground black pepper

8 hamburger buns

1. In the Dutch oven over medium heat, heat the olive oil. Add the onion and cook for 3 minutes. Add the ground beef and cook, breaking up the meat, until all the pink is gone, about 15 minutes.

2. Add the tomato sauce and Worcestershire sauce. Reduce the heat to low, partially cover, and simmer for 25 minutes. Season with salt and pepper.

3. Cut the buns in half and scoop a large spoonful or two of sloppy joe onto each bun bottom. Top each with the remaining bun half and enjoy.

COOK IT SLOW: You can also make sloppy joes in a slow cooker. Simply add all of the ingredients (except the buns) to the slow cooker. Use a spatula to break up the meat, then cook on high for 4 hours.

PER SERVING Calories: 330; Total Fat: 19g; Saturated Fat: 7g; Cholesterol: 43mg; Sodium: 465mg; Total Carbohydrates: 24g; Sugars: 5g; Protein: 14g

Skirt Steak Sandwiches

DUTCH OVEN • 10-INCH SKILLET

DAIRY-FREE • NUT-FREE

I'm all about sandwiches for dinner—especially when they involve juicy, pan-seared steak, quick-sautéed tomatoes and onions, and crusty baguette. Make sure to pat the steak dry before seasoning. If you don't, moisture on its surface will prevent the steak from developing the flavorful caramelized crust that makes it so mouthwatering.

SERVES 2
PREP TIME: 5 MINUTES
COOK TIME: 20 MINUTES

1 pound skirt steak

2 teaspoons ground cumin

Salt

Freshly ground black pepper

4 tablespoons extra-virgin olive oil, divided

1 small onion, thinly sliced

2 roma tomatoes, quartered

2 baguettes, slit lengthwise

1. Pat the steak dry with paper towels, and season with the cumin, salt, and pepper.

2. In the Dutch oven over medium-high heat, heat 2 tablespoons of olive oil. Sear each side of the steak for 5 minutes. Transfer to a cutting board and let it rest for 10 minutes. Thinly slice across the grain into ½- to ¾-inch-wide strips.

3. In the Dutch oven, heat the remaining 2 tablespoons of olive oil. Add the onion and tomatoes and cook for 3 to 4 minutes, until the onions begin to wilt. Season with salt and pepper. Return the steak to the pan. Mix and remove from the heat.

4. Place a few slices of the steak mixture inside each of the baguettes and serve.

COOKWARE SWAP: You can also pan sear this skirt steak in a 10-inch skillet, using the same recipe instructions.

PER SERVING Calories: 790; Total Fat: 33g; Saturated Fat: 9g; Cholesterol: 100mg; Sodium: 842mg; Total Carbohydrates: 63g; Sugars: 7g; Protein: 59g

Comforting Red Wine Steak

DUTCH OVEN

DAIRY-FREE · GLUTEN-FREE · NUT-FREE

Red wine is one of those "hero" ingredients that can turn an ordinary meal into something extraordinary. Pairing it with steak is a no-brainer. Here it is reduced along with the drippings from the steak, shallots, and fresh thyme. This is a restaurant-quality dish that is dead easy to make at home. You don't need to splurge for an expensive wine, but do choose one that's good enough to drink on its own.

SERVES 2
PREP TIME: 5 MINUTES
COOK TIME: 40 MINUTES

2 (8-ounce) sirloin steaks, trimmed of fat

Salt

Freshly ground black pepper

4 tablespoons extra-virgin olive oil, divided

1 pound fingerling potatoes, rinsed, halved

3 tablespoons shallots, minced

2 teaspoons chopped fresh thyme

¾ cup red wine

1. Pat the steaks dry with a paper towel. Season generously with salt and pepper. Let them rest at room temperature for 15 to 20 minutes before cooking.

2. Meanwhile, in the Dutch oven over medium heat, heat 1 tablespoon of olive oil. Add the potatoes, season with salt and pepper, and toss well. Cover the pot tightly and cook over low heat for 20 to 30 minutes, until the potatoes are fork-tender. Set aside.

3. Heat the Dutch oven over high heat. Add the remaining 3 tablespoons of oil, then lower the heat to medium-high. Add the steaks and cook for 4 minutes on each side for medium-rare, or longer as desired. Remove from the pot and set aside.

4. Add the shallots and thyme to the pot. Add the wine and cook until the liquid is almost evaporated, 1 to 2 minutes. Season with salt and pepper, and stir with a whisk.

5. Spoon the sauce over the steaks, and serve with the potatoes.

PREP TIP: Clean your potatoes by scrubbing with a firm, soft brush under running cold water to remove the dirt from the skin.

PER SERVING Calories: 742; Total Fat: 32g; Saturated Fat: 7g; Cholesterol: 152mg; Sodium: 210mg; Total Carbohydrates: 42g; Sugars: 3g; Protein: 56g

Steak Seared in Browned Butter

DUTCH OVEN

GLUTEN-FREE • NUT-FREE

Browned butter, also called *beurre noisette*, is a magical ingredient that is easy to make from regular unsalted butter. To make it, you cook the butter until the water evaporates and the milk solids caramelize and turn brown. As if butter wasn't already one of the most delicious things on the planet, browning it makes it even better. It develops an intensely rich, nutty flavor that is the perfect match for seared steak and potatoes.

SERVES 4
PREP TIME: 10 MINUTES
COOK TIME: 20 MINUTES,
PLUS 30 MINUTES TO REST

2 (1-pound) steaks,
1 inch thick

1 tablespoon extra-virgin
olive oil

3 tablespoons unsalted
butter, divided

1 pound Yukon gold potatoes,
sliced about ½ inch thick

2 fresh rosemary sprigs

Salt

Freshly ground black pepper

½ cup beef broth

1. Let the steaks rest at room temperature for 30 minutes.

2. Meanwhile, in the Dutch oven over medium-high heat, heat the oil and 1 tablespoon of butter. Add the potatoes and rosemary and cook for 5 minutes, until fork-tender. Season with salt and pepper. Remove from the pot and set aside.

3. Season the steak generously with salt and pepper. Add the steak to the Dutch oven over high heat and cook for 5 minutes on each side for medium-rare, or longer if desired. Remove the steaks and let them rest on a cutting board.

4. Melt the remaining 2 tablespoons of butter over medium heat, stirring often. Add the broth when the butter starts to brown. Keep stirring and scraping up the browned bits using a wooden spoon.

5. Add the potatoes to the pan and heat through, about 5 minutes. Cut the steaks in half, spoon the potatoes and browned butter over each steak, and serve.

INGREDIENT TIP: Resting the steaks at room temperature promotes more even cooking. But if you forget, dry them very thoroughly with paper towels before searing.

PER SERVING Calories: 532; Total Fat: 24g; Saturated Fat: 10g; Cholesterol: 188mg; Sodium: 324mg; Total Carbohydrates: 18g; Sugars: 1g; Protein: 58g

Sheet Pan

5

A sheet pan, sometimes called a baking sheet, is a rectangular, flat metal pan (usually aluminum or stainless steel) with a 1-inch lip. It goes in the oven and is typically used for baking pastries, bread rolls, cookies, Swiss rolls, sheet cakes, and pizzas, but it can also be used for baking or roasting pork chops, salmon, veggies, and chicken, to name a few.

Sheet pans are available in a variety of sizes, but the two most common sizes are full, which is 26 by 18 inches, and half, which is 18 by 13 inches. For home cooking, a half sheet pan is ideal, as a full sheet pan is too big for most home ovens.

Sheet pan meals are perfect when cooking for a crowd. The recipes are so easy, and they can easily be adjusted to include any ingredients that are in season or happen to be in your pantry. Still, you don't just dump all the ingredients onto the pan and pop it into the oven. There are a few tricks to making a great sheet pan dinner.

Spicy Shrimp and Veggies, page 89

- **Invest in a good sheet pan.** I recommend stainless steel or aluminum pans, which are nice and sturdy and last forever if you take care of them. Buy the best one you can. While stainless steel is more durable, it can be a poor conductor of heat, so make sure you purchase a higher-end one. Acidic foods degrade aluminum and can leach into food, so avoid using aluminum pans for highly acidic foods, such as tomato, unless the pan has been anodized (coated with a protective oxide layer).

- **Line the pan with either aluminum foil or parchment paper before cooking** to help make cleanup easy. Parchment paper has nonstick properties. If you use foil, be careful not to end up with a little piece stuck to the bottom of your food.

- **If you're broiling, do not use parchment paper,** which can catch fire. Go with the foil and mist it with nonstick cooking spray to prevent food from sticking.

- **Get to know your oven.** Every oven is different. Buying a cheap oven thermometer can help keep you (and your oven) honest. Turning the pan around halfway through cooking helps make hot spots a non-issue.

- **Food pieces that are different sizes can take different times to cook,** so always start with the biggest items that take the longest to cook, such as meat or potatoes, and add smaller items to the pan later.

- **Cut vegetables to the same shape and size,** and cut meat portions to the same thickness, so they will cook evenly.

- **Arrange things on the sheet thoughtfully for the best results.** Place the protein in the center of the pan so it will absorb the most heat, then scatter your vegetables around it. Don't overcrowd; if food is packed too tightly, any moisture that's released won't evaporate—giving you soggy results.

- Baked fries can turn out limp. **Presoak your cut fries in water** for 30 minutes for russet potatoes and 45 minutes for sweet potatoes before you coat them in olive oil and bake in the oven. This will pull the starch out of the potatoes' fibers, which reduces the internal water content so your fries will bake up nice and crisp.

Not-Your-Usual Caesar Salad

EXTRA-QUICK · NUT-FREE · VEGETARIAN

Roasting romaine lettuce may seem strange, but try it once and you'll understand. High heat caramelizes the sugars in the leafy green just the way it does for other roasted vegetables. This very well may become your favorite recipe for a fast, no-fuss, healthy, and light meal.

SERVES 4
PREP TIME: 5 MINUTES
COOK TIME: 10 MINUTES

Nonstick cooking spray

2 large romaine lettuce hearts, halved lengthwise

2 tablespoons extra-virgin olive oil, divided

1 garlic clove, finely chopped

Salt

Freshly ground black pepper

8 whole-wheat baguette slices

¼ cup grated Parmesan cheese

Juice of 1 lemon

1. Preheat the oven to 400°F. Lightly coat the sheet pan with nonstick cooking spray.

2. Arrange the romaine lettuce halves cut-side down on the sheet pan. Coat with 1 tablespoon of olive oil, and sprinkle with the garlic. Season with salt and pepper.

3. Brush both sides of the bread slices with the remaining 1 tablespoon of oil. Place the bread on the pan. Bake for 8 to 10 minutes, or until the lettuce is browned and the edges of the bread are golden.

4. Divide the lettuce and bread slices evenly among four plates. Top with the Parmesan cheese, sprinkle with the lemon juice, and serve.

VARIATION: For authentic flavor, add 2 oil-packed anchovy fillets. Drain the oil, chop the anchovy fillets, then add with the 1 tablespoon of oil in step 3.

PER SERVING Calories: 274; Total Fat: 10g; Saturated Fat: 2g; Cholesterol: 5mg; Sodium: 522mg; Total Carbohydrates: 37g; Sugars: 2g; Protein: 10g

Super Loaded Baked Sweet Potato

DAIRY-FREE · GLUTEN-FREE · NUT-FREE · VEGAN

Tender, sweet roasted sweet potatoes are tossed with black beans, cherry tomatoes, red onion, and lime for a fresh spin on a loaded baked potato. As is, it makes a satisfying light meal, but you could make it heartier by adding your favorite chili-style toppings, like shredded cheese, guacamole, or sour cream.

SERVES 4
PREP TIME: 10 MINUTES
COOK TIME: 20 MINUTES

Nonstick cooking spray

4 medium sweet potatoes, peeled and diced

3 tablespoons extra-virgin olive oil

Salt

Freshly ground black pepper

1 (15-ounce) can black beans, rinsed and drained

2 cups cherry tomatoes, halved

1 small red onion, diced

Zest and juice of 1 lime

Optional garnish:

¼ cup chopped fresh cilantro

1. Preheat the oven to 400°F. Lightly spray the sheet pan with nonstick cooking spray.

2. In a large mixing bowl, toss the sweet potatoes with the olive oil, and season with salt and pepper. Spread out in a single layer on the pan and bake for 20 minutes, or until the potatoes are starting to brown.

3. In a large serving bowl, combine the cooked sweet potatoes, black beans, tomatoes, red onion, and the lime zest and juice. Season with salt and pepper, and toss to combine. Sprinkle with the cilantro, if using, and serve.

PREP TIP: To cook this dish faster, dice the sweet potatoes into smaller pieces.

PER SERVING Calories: 312; Total Fat: 11g; Saturated Fat: 2g; Cholesterol: 0mg; Sodium: 98mg; Total Carbohydrates: 45g; Sugars: 7g; Protein: 10g

Baked Salmon with Zesty Salad

SHEET PAN

DAIRY-FREE • GLUTEN-FREE • NUT-FREE

I've made this dish dozens of times, and I still can't get over how so few ingredients can create such a flavorful and satisfying dish. Roasted salmon is meaty and delicious, and the zesty salad and mango salsa are delightfully bright counterpoints to the fatty fish.

SERVES 4
PREP TIME: 10 MINUTES
COOK TIME: 30 MINUTES

Nonstick cooking spray

4 (5-ounce) skin-on salmon fillets

5 tablespoons extra-virgin olive oil, divided

Salt

Freshly ground black pepper

1 cup peeled, pitted, and cubed mango

1 jalapeño, seeded and minced

Zest of 1 lime

Juice of ½ lime

3 cups mixed salad greens, such as arugula, kale, and spinach

1. Preheat the oven to 350°F. Lightly spray the sheet pan with nonstick cooking spray.

2. Brush the salmon with 1 tablespoon of olive oil, and season with salt and pepper on both sides. Place the salmon on the sheet pan skin-side down, and bake for 25 minutes. Flip and continue to bake on the other side for 5 minutes.

3. In a medium mixing bowl, combine the mango and jalapeño, season with salt and pepper, and mix in 2 tablespoons of olive oil and the lime zest. Set aside.

4. In a large mixing bowl, toss the mixed salad greens with the remaining 2 tablespoon of olive oil and the lime juice. Season with salt and pepper. Set aside.

5. To assemble, serve the salmon on a plate topped with the mango salsa with the salad on the side.

INGREDIENT TIP: When buying salmon, always look for the most vibrant color and flesh that appears moist—these are signs of freshness. For this dish, frozen salmon fillets are also okay.

PER SERVING Calories: 438; Total Fat: 32g; Saturated Fat: 6g; Cholesterol: 85mg; Sodium: 173mg; Total Carbohydrates: 9g; Sugars: 6g; Protein: 29g

Salmon with Zucchini and Cherry Tomatoes

SHEET PAN · 10-INCH SKILLET

DAIRY-FREE · GLUTEN-FREE · NUT-FREE

Ancho powder is a chili powder made of ground dried red-brown ancho chiles (before drying, these green chiles are called poblanos). These chiles are both sweet and slightly hot. Ancho powder has a deeper, richer flavor than a standard chili powder, which is usually a combination of mild dried ground chiles, cumin, oregano, and other flavors. You'll find ancho powder among the spices in many supermarkets or at any Latin food market.

SERVES 4
PREP TIME: 5 MINUTES
COOK TIME: 30 MINUTES

Nonstick cooking spray

4 (5-ounce) skin-on salmon fillets

2 tablespoons extra-virgin olive oil, divided

Salt

Freshly ground black pepper

2 cups cubed zucchini

2 cups cherry tomatoes

1 teaspoon ancho chili powder

1. Preheat the oven to 350°F. Lightly spray the sheet pan with nonstick cooking spray.

2. Brush the salmon with 1 tablespoon of olive oil, and season with salt and pepper on both sides. Place skin-side down on the sheet pan.

3. In a large bowl, combine the zucchini, cherry tomatoes, ancho chili powder, and the remaining 1 tablespoon of olive oil. Season with salt and pepper and toss well. Arrange the zucchini and tomatoes around the salmon.

4. Bake for 25 minutes. Flip and continue to cook on the other side for 5 minutes. Serve each fillet surrounded by roasted veggies.

COOKWARE SWAP: You can also make this dish in a 10-inch skillet. Place the seasoned salmon skin-side down in the skillet, and add the rest of the ingredients around the salmon. Cook over medium heat for 5 minutes, then flip the salmon and cook for another 5 minutes, or until the salmon can be flaked with a fork. Transfer the salmon to a serving plate, and continue cooking the veggies for another 3 to 5 minutes, or until the zucchini is tender.

PER SERVING Calories: 339; Total Fat: 23g; Saturated Fat: 4g; Cholesterol: 85mg; Sodium: 141mg; Total Carbohydrates: 6g; Sugars: 4g; Protein: 30g

Thai Glazed Salmon

DAIRY-FREE • GLUTEN-FREE • NUT-FREE

Thai sweet chili sauce is a mixture of rice vinegar, hot peppers, and sugar cooked together to make a sweet-spicy sauce. You can buy it in bottles in the international foods aisle of many supermarkets or in an Asian food market. If you like, serve this salmon with steamed white or brown rice, or over a bed of chopped fresh lettuce.

SERVES 4
PREP TIME: 5 MINUTES
COOK TIME: 25 MINUTES

4 (5-ounce) skin-on
salmon fillets

2 cups green beans, trimmed

½ cup Thai sweet chili sauce

¼ cup soy sauce

Juice of 1 lime

Optional garnish:

Chopped fresh cilantro

Lime slices

1. Preheat the oven to 375°F. Line the sheet pan with aluminum foil.

2. Place the salmon on the pan skin-side down. Scatter the green beans around the salmon.

3. In a small bowl, combine the sweet chili sauce, soy sauce, and lime juice. Drizzle half the sauce over the salmon and green beans. Fold the foil over the salmon and green beans, making sure they are completely covered, and bake for 15 to 20 minutes.

4. Carefully open the foil, brush everything with some of the remaining sauce, and broil for 5 minutes, or until the top starts to blacken. Remove from the oven.

5. Brush the top of the salmon with the remaining sauce. Garnish with the cilantro and lime slices, if using, and serve.

VARIATION: If your grocery store does not carry Thai sweet chili sauce, try substituting 1 tablespoon of sriracha sauce and 1 tablespoon of honey. The taste will be slightly different, but it will still deliver amazing sweet heat.

PER SERVING Calories: 415; Total Fat: 18g; Saturated Fat: 5g;
Cholesterol: 69mg; Sodium: 1,219mg; Total Carbohydrates: 19g;
Sugars: 13g; Protein: 35g

Honey-Mustard Salmon and Veggies

SHEET PAN

DAIRY-FREE · GLUTEN-FREE · NUT-FREE

This is another super simple recipe that elevates salmon and veggies to a whole new level. Equal parts honey and Dijon mustard make a quick sweet-savory sauce. Along with roasted zucchini, this salmon makes a colorful, healthy, and satisfying dinner that you can put on the table fast.

SERVES 4
PREP TIME: 5 MINUTES
COOK TIME: 15 MINUTES

4 (5-ounce) skinless
salmon fillets

1 pound zucchini, chopped

3 tablespoons extra-virgin
olive oil, divided

Salt

Freshly ground black pepper

1 cup honey

1 cup Dijon mustard

Optional garnish:

2 tablespoons chopped
fresh parsley

¼ teaspoon red pepper flakes

1. Preheat the oven to 400°F. Line the sheet pan with parchment paper.

2. Lay the salmon fillets on one side of the sheet pan and the zucchini on the other. Toss 1 tablespoon of olive oil with the zucchini, and season with salt and pepper.

3. In a small bowl, combine the honey, mustard, and the remaining 2 tablespoons of olive oil. Generously brush each salmon piece with this mustard glaze.

4. Bake for 12 to 15 minutes, or until the salmon flakes easily with a fork.

5. To serve, brush another layer of mustard glaze on the salmon. Garnish the fish with fresh parsley, if using, and sprinkle red pepper flakes over the zucchini, if desired, and serve.

INGREDIENT TIP: To pick the best zucchini, choose those that are shiny, firm, and vibrant in color with no spots, cuts, or bruises. Larger zucchini are best for baking because they are firm in texture and take longer to cook over the stove top.

PER SERVING Calories: 526; Total Fat: 24g; Saturated Fat: 4g; Cholesterol: 84mg; Sodium: 490mg; Total Carbohydrates: 40g; Sugars: 37g; Protein: 40g

Fish Gremolata

DAIRY-FREE · GLUTEN-FREE · NUT-FREE

Gremolata is an uncooked Italian condiment used to finish everything from braised meats to grilled fish. It's beautiful in its simplicity; the classic recipe combines minced garlic, parsley, and lemon zest. Spooned over cooked meat, fish, or vegetables, it makes the simplest of dishes pop with bright, fresh flavor. I love it with roasted cod and cherry tomatoes.

SERVES 4 to 6
PREP TIME: 10 MINUTES
COOK TIME: 20 MINUTES

Nonstick cooking spray

6 (4- to 6-ounce) skinless cod fillets

4 tablespoons extra-virgin olive oil, divided

Salt

Freshly ground black pepper

1 small bunch parsley

1 garlic clove

Juice of 1 lemon

3 cups cherry tomatoes, combination of colors

1. Preheat the oven to 450°F. Lightly coat the sheet pan with nonstick cooking spray.

2. Arrange the cod on the sheet pan. Drizzle with 2 tablespoons of olive oil, and season with salt and pepper. Bake for 10 minutes.

3. While the fish is cooking, make the sauce. Finely chop the parsley and garlic, and transfer to a small bowl. Stir in the lemon juice, and season with salt and pepper.

4. Remove the fish from the oven, and arrange the cherry tomatoes on the pan around the fish. Drizzle with the remaining 2 tablespoons of olive oil, and return the pan to the oven. Bake for another 10 minutes, or until the fish flakes easily with a fork and the tomatoes are beginning to burst.

5. To serve, spoon the sauce over the fish.

INGREDIENT TIP: Fresh cod doesn't have much of a fishy smell. It should always be fresh, not frozen, or it will end up mushy. You could also use any firm white fish fillets, such as tilapia.

PER SERVING Calories: 284; Total Fat: 16g; Saturated Fat: 2g; Cholesterol: 83mg; Sodium: 155mg; Total Carbohydrates: 6g; Sugars: 4g; Protein: 32g

Sheet Pan Cajun Shrimp

SHEET PAN

DAIRY-FREE · GLUTEN-FREE · NUT-FREE

With a cold beer in one hand and this Cajun shrimp in another, you have the perfect meal for a quick game-day dinner while cheering your favorite team on to victory. The bell peppers and corn add a sweet counterpoint to the smoky sausage.

SERVES 4
PREP TIME: 5 MINUTES
COOK TIME: 20 MINUTES

1 pound large shrimp, peeled and deveined

1 (12.8-ounce) package smoked andouille sausage, sliced

2 bell peppers, seeded and chopped into chunks

3 ears corn, each cut into 6 pieces

2 tablespoons Cajun seasoning

2 tablespoons extra-virgin olive oil

Salt

Freshly ground black pepper

1. Preheat the oven to 400°F.

2. In a large bowl, combine the shrimp, sausage, bell peppers, corn, Cajun seasoning, and olive oil. Season with salt and pepper, and toss until everything is well coated. Spread evenly on the sheet pan.

3. Bake for 20 minutes, or until the shrimp is pink and the vegetables are tender, and serve.

VARIATION: Don't like or can't find andouille sausage? Substitute bratwurst or any smoked sausage.

PER SERVING Calories: 443; Total Fat: 25g; Saturated Fat: 8g; Cholesterol: 221mg; Sodium: 867mg; Total Carbohydrates: 18g; Sugars: 5g; Protein: 39g

Spicy Shrimp and Veggies

DAIRY-FREE · GLUTEN-FREE · NUT-FREE

Cajun or Creole seasoning is a spicy mixture of garlic powder, dried thyme, cayenne, and other herbs and spices. Seasoning mixes like this are great for quick-cook meals since they pack a ton of flavors into one product. Toss it with shrimp, veggies, and a couple of other kitchen staples for a sheet pan meal that will appeal to the whole family.

SERVES 4
PREP TIME: 10 MINUTES
COOK TIME: 20 MINUTES,
PLUS 30 MINUTES TO
MARINATE

1 cup extra-virgin olive oil

4 tablespoons Cajun or Creole seasoning

4 tablespoons chopped fresh parsley

2 tablespoons honey

Dash salt

1 pound large shrimp, peeled and deveined

2 pounds mixed vegetables, such as broccoli, zucchini, and squash, diced

Optional garnish:

Lemon wedges

1. In a large bowl, combine the olive oil, seasoning, parsley, honey, and salt. Transfer half of the mixture to another large bowl, add the shrimp to it, and refrigerate for 30 minutes.

2. Preheat the oven to 450°F.

3. Add the vegetables to the other bowl, and toss to combine. Spread the vegetables in a single layer on the sheet pan. Bake for 12 to 15 minutes. Add the shrimp and bake for 5 minutes, or until the shrimp are just opaque and the vegetables are tender and golden around the edges.

4. Serve with lemon wedges, if using.

VARIATION: Add any leftovers to your favorite cooked pasta for lunch the next day. Toss the pasta with olive oil to prevent sticking.

PER SERVING Calories: 437; Total Fat: 25g; Saturated Fat: 4g; Cholesterol: 162mg; Sodium: 1,185mg; Total Carbohydrates: 30g; Sugars: 15g; Protein: 25g

Thin-Crust Clam Pizza

SHEET PAN

EXTRA-QUICK · NUT-FREE

Clam pizza is a beloved regional specialty in New England, but you can easily replicate it wherever you live. Use canned clams and store-bought pizza crust and you can have it ready in way less time than it would take to order a pizza and have it delivered.

SERVES 4
PREP TIME: 5 MINUTES
COOK TIME: 10 MINUTES

Nonstick cooking spray

1 store-bought cooked thin pizza crust

2 tablespoons extra-virgin olive oil

2 cups shredded mozzarella cheese

1 (10-ounce) can whole clams, drained

1 tablespoon Old Bay seasoning

2 cups baby arugula

Optional garnish:

2 tablespoons thinly sliced fresh basil

Red pepper flakes

1. Preheat the oven to 425°F. Lightly coat the sheet pan with nonstick cooking spray.

2. Place the crust on the sheet pan. Lightly coat it with olive oil, and sprinkle with the cheese.

3. In a small bowl, toss the clams in the seasoning. Evenly distribute them over the pizza.

4. Bake for 10 minutes, or until the crust is light brown. Top with the arugula. Garnish with basil and red pepper flakes, if using, and serve.

VARIATION: If you decide to use raw pizza dough, knead the dough about 6 times on a lightly floured surface, then brush it with olive oil. Roll and stretch into a 12-inch round. Bake for 10 minutes at 450°F, then follow steps 2 and 3. You can also substitute flatbread for the pizza crust.

PER SERVING Calories: 375; Total Fat: 24g; Saturated Fat: 5g; Cholesterol: 37mg; Sodium: 944mg; Total Carbohydrates: 30g; Sugars: 1g; Protein: 14g

Arugula and Prosciutto Pizza

NUT-FREE

This quick recipe delivers excellent flavor in just 25 minutes. It's hard to believe that this pizza could pack such a punch while also being ready so quickly. If you drink wine, try pairing this with an Italian Chianti or another light red wine.

SERVES 4
PREP TIME: 5 MINUTES
COOK TIME: 20 MINUTES

Nonstick cooking spray

1 store-bought cooked pizza crust

1 (14.5-ounce) can fire-roasted diced tomatoes, drained

2 cups shredded mozzarella cheese

4 ounces sliced prosciutto

2 cups arugula

1. Preheat the oven to 450°F. Lightly coat the sheet pan with nonstick cooking spray.

2. Place the pizza crust on the sheet pan. Spoon the fire-roasted tomatoes onto the crust, and sprinkle the cheese over the top.

3. Bake for 20 minutes. Remove from the oven and top with the prosciutto and arugula. Serve immediately.

INGREDIENT TIP: See Thin-Crust Clam Pizza (page 90) for tips on using raw pizza dough. To prevent prosciutto from drying out, cover the packaging tightly with plastic wrap and keep in the refrigerator.

PER SERVING Calories: 306; Total Fat: 14g; Saturated Fat: 5g; Cholesterol: 33mg; Sodium: 1,138mg; Total Carbohydrates: 31g; Sugars: 3g; Protein: 17g

Buffalo Chicken Pizza

SHEET PAN

EXTRA-QUICK · NUT-FREE

There's easy, and then there's really easy. And this delicious, smoky, spicy, cheesy Buffalo chicken pizza is really easy. This pizza never fails to impress when I need something quick and easy that my friends and family will love.

SERVES 4
PREP TIME: 5 MINUTES
COOK TIME: 10 MINUTES

Nonstick cooking spray

1 store-bought cooked pizza crust

¾ cup Monterey Jack cheese

1 cup cubed cooked rotisserie chicken

1 tablespoon store-bought hot wing sauce

½ cup chopped pineapple

Optional garnish:

Chopped fresh parsley

1. Preheat the oven to 450°F. Lightly coat the sheet pan with nonstick cooking spray.

2. Place the crust on the sheet pan, then spread the cheese all over the crust. In a medium bowl, toss the chicken in the hot wing sauce, then scatter it over the cheese.

3. Bake for 8 to 10 minutes, or until the crust is golden brown and the cheese has melted. Remove from the oven and top with the pineapple. Sprinkle the parsley, if using, on top. Serve immediately.

VARIATION: See Thin-Crust Clam Pizza (page 90) for tips on using raw pizza dough.

PER SERVING Calories: 314; Total Fat: 12g; Saturated Fat: 5g; Cholesterol: 46mg; Sodium: 431mg; Total Carbohydrates: 31g; Sugars: 3g; Protein: 21g

Lemon Chicken with Asparagus

SHEET PAN

DAIRY-FREE • NUT-FREE

Take advantage of seasonal vegetables when you can! This dish has a variety of textures and flavors that bring out the best in each ingredient. Lemon and honey brighten up simple chicken breast, and asparagus adds color, texture, and freshness.

SERVES 4
PREP TIME: 10 MINUTES
COOK TIME: 35 MINUTES

Nonstick cooking spray

6 tablespoons extra-virgin olive oil, divided

½ cup honey

1 tablespoon soy sauce

4 boneless, skinless chicken breasts

Salt

Freshly ground black pepper

1 lemon, sliced

1 bunch asparagus (20 to 30 spears), trimmed

1. Preheat the oven to 400°F. Line the sheet pan with aluminum foil and lightly spray with nonstick cooking spray.

2. In a small bowl, combine 5 tablespoons of olive oil with the honey and soy sauce.

3. Season the chicken with salt and pepper. Arrange on the sheet pan, and place the lemon slices over the top of the chicken. Generously brush the oil mixture all over the chicken, reserving some for later. Wrap the foil over the chicken and bake for 20 minutes.

4. Open the foil. Arrange the asparagus on one side of the pan, coat with the remaining 1 tablespoon of olive oil, and season with salt and pepper. Brush the chicken with another coat of the oil mixture.

5. Return to the oven and bake until the chicken is golden and the asparagus is cooked, about 15 minutes, and serve.

VARIATION: Get creative. Turn any leftover chicken into a sandwich; thinly slice the chicken and serve it on multigrain bread with scallions and sriracha.

PER SERVING Calories: 478; Total Fat: 23g; Saturated Fat: 3g; Cholesterol: 65mg; Sodium: 345mg; Total Carbohydrates: 44g; Sugars: 39g; Protein: 31g

Chicken Parmesan

SHEET PAN

NUT-FREE

Chicken Parmesan is one of my guilty pleasures. For a change of pace, I sometimes cut the chicken into bite-size pieces and turn it into popcorn chicken, which is a perfect dish to munch in front of the TV for movie night!

SERVES 4 to 6
PREP TIME: 5 MINUTES
COOK TIME: 25 MINUTES,
PLUS 30 MINUTES TO
MARINATE

6 boneless, skinless
chicken breasts

2 cups buttermilk

Nonstick cooking spray

1 cup Italian breadcrumbs

⅔ cup grated
Parmesan cheese

4 cups broccoli florets

2 tablespoons extra-virgin
olive oil

Salt

1. Put the chicken breasts and buttermilk in a large zip-top plastic bag, and knead several times to coat the chicken with buttermilk. Squeeze the air from the bag, seal, and refrigerate for 30 minutes.

2. Preheat the oven to 400°F. Lightly coat the sheet pan with nonstick cooking spray.

3. In a small bowl, combine the breadcrumbs and Parmesan cheese. Dip each chicken breast into the breadcrumb mixture.

4. Arrange the coated chicken breasts on the sheet pan and top with any remaining breadcrumb mixture. Bake for 15 minutes.

5. While the chicken is cooking, wash the broccoli and dry very thoroughly. Coat well with the olive oil, and sprinkle with salt. Spread the broccoli in a single layer around the chicken. Return to the oven and bake for 10 minutes more, or until the chicken pieces are no longer pink inside and the coating is crisp, and serve.

VARIATION: Feeling creative tonight? Crush up 30 saltine crackers and use them instead of the breadcrumbs.

PER SERVING Calories: 484; Total Fat: 16g; Saturated Fat: 5g; Cholesterol: 115mg; Sodium: 670mg; Total Carbohydrates: 32g; Sugars: 9g; Protein: 54g

Garlic-Parmesan Chicken Wings

GLUTEN-FREE · NUT-FREE

This bar-food favorite is begging for your attention! Baking instead of frying makes this dish so much lighter and less oily, not to mention a whole lot less labor-intensive to cook and clean up after. The next time you have friends over to watch a game, this should definitely be on your menu.

SERVES 4
PREP TIME: 10 MINUTES
COOK TIME: 30 MINUTES

Nonstick cooking spray

1 pound chicken wings

4 tablespoons extra-virgin olive oil, divided

Salt

Freshly ground black pepper

4 russet potatoes, scrubbed and cut into eighths

4 whole garlic cloves

8 tablespoons (1 stick) unsalted butter, melted

1 cup grated Parmesan cheese, plus more for garnish

Optional garnish:

1 tablespoon red pepper flakes

1. Preheat the oven to 450°F. Lightly coat the sheet pan with nonstick cooking spray.

2. In a large bowl, toss the chicken wings in 2 tablespoons of olive oil and season with salt and pepper. Arrange the wings in a single layer on the sheet pan. In the same bowl, toss the potatoes and garlic with the remaining 2 tablespoons of olive oil, season with salt and pepper, then spread them out on the sheet pan around the chicken.

3. Bake for 12 to 15 minutes, then flip the wings over and cook 10 to 15 minutes more, until the wings are browned and cooked through and the potatoes are golden and crispy. Remove from the oven and place the wings on a large serving plate.

4. In a small bowl, combine the melted butter with the roasted garlic and the Parmesan cheese. Pour the butter over the chicken. Sprinkle with more cheese and the red pepper flakes, if using, and serve with the potatoes on the side.

PREP TIP: To melt butter in a microwave, place it in a microwave-safe dish and melt on high uncovered for 30 to 45 seconds. Repeat for another 15 to 30 seconds, if needed.

PER SERVING Calories: 538; Total Fat: 49g; Saturated Fat: 18g; Cholesterol: 156mg; Sodium: 571mg; Total Carbohydrates: 2g; Sugars: 0g; Protein: 26g

Chimichurri Chicken

SHEET PAN

DAIRY-FREE · GLUTEN-FREE · NUT-FREE

Chimichurri is a bright and flavorful sauce that is essential to Argentinian cuisine. Beef-loving Argentinian chefs usually serve it over grilled steak, but I love the fresh, raw sauce over oven-roasted chicken. I also love that you can make a batch of this sauce, stash it in the refrigerator, and use it for up to 2 weeks.

SERVES 8
PREP TIME: 10 MINUTES
COOK TIME: 50 MINUTES

Nonstick cooking spray

8 bone-in chicken thighs or breasts

1½ cups extra-virgin olive oil, divided

Salt

Freshly ground black pepper

1½ pounds red potatoes, halved

4 garlic cloves

1 cup chopped fresh flatleaf parsley

1 cup fresh cilantro

Optional garnish:

¼ teaspoon red pepper flakes

1. Preheat the oven to 400°F. Lightly coat the sheet pan with nonstick cooking spray.

2. Arrange the chicken on the sheet pan. Toss with 1 tablespoon of olive oil, and season with salt and pepper. Arrange the potatoes on the sheet pan around the chicken. Coat with 1 tablespoon of olive oil, and season with salt and pepper.

3. Bake for 45 to 50 minutes, or until the chicken juices run clear and the potatoes are tender.

4. While the chicken is cooking, make the chimichurri sauce. In a food processor, combine the garlic, parsley, cilantro, and the remaining olive oil. Pulse until combined but not smooth. Season with salt and pepper.

5. Transfer the chicken and potatoes to a large serving plate, and drizzle with the chimichurri sauce. Sprinkle on the pepper flakes, if using, and serve.

PREP TIP: I like having chimichurri sauce handy. And it's also perfect to pair with baked salmon or skirt steak. Make up a batch and store it in an airtight jar in the refrigerator for up to 2 weeks. For a spicy kick, you can also add jalapeño into the food processor.

PER SERVING Calories: 386; Total Fat: 23g; Saturated Fat: 3g; Cholesterol: 90mg; Sodium: 101mg; Total Carbohydrates: 14g; Sugars: 1g; Protein: 32g

Chicken Tacos

SHEET PAN

DAIRY-FREE · GLUTEN-FREE · NUT-FREE

Upgrade your #TacoTuesday dinner with these chicken tacos. Chicken tenders are tossed on a sheet pan with olive oil and seasonings and then roasted with peppers and onions for a fun tortilla filling. These tacos make a perfectly balanced meal that I could easily eat once a week.

SERVES 4
PREP TIME: 5 MINUTES
COOK TIME: 20 MINUTES,
PLUS 30 MINUTES TO
MARINATE

1½ pounds chicken tenders, quartered

4 tablespoons extra-virgin olive oil, divided

1½ teaspoons ground cumin

Salt

Freshly ground black pepper,

Nonstick cooking spray

3 bell peppers, assorted colors, seeded and thinly sliced

1 onion, thinly sliced

12 corn tortillas, warmed

Optional garnish:

Lime wedges

Fresh cilantro

1. Season the chicken with 2 tablespoons of olive oil and the cumin, salt, and pepper. Put the chicken in a zip-top bag and marinate in the refrigerator for 30 minutes.

2. Preheat the oven to 400°F. Lightly coat the sheet pan with nonstick cooking spray.

3. Spread the chicken mixture on the sheet pan, and arrange the bell peppers and onion around it. Toss with the remaining 2 tablespoons of olive oil, and season with salt and pepper. Bake for 15 to 20 minutes, until the chicken is no longer pink.

4. Divide the chicken and vegetables among four plates and serve with corn tortillas, and garnish with lime wedges and fresh cilantro, if using.

VARIATION: If you can't find chicken tenders, you can slice boneless, skinless chicken breasts into strips.

PER SERVING Calories: 509; Total Fat: 19g; Saturated Fat: 2g; Cholesterol: 98mg; Sodium: 192mg; Total Carbohydrates: 42g; Sugars: 6g; Protein: 44g

Chicken Cordon Bleu

SHEET PAN

FREEZER-FRIENDLY · NUT-FREE

Chicken cordon bleu is a favorite European classic preparation of chicken breast in which the breast is stuffed with smoky ham and Swiss cheese, breaded, and fried. It is usually somewhat painstaking to make, but this recipe makes it super easy by layering the cheese and ham on top of the chicken, rolling it up, and then baking it in the oven instead of frying it.

SERVES 4
PREP TIME: 10 MINUTES
COOK TIME: 30 MINUTES

Nonstick cooking spray

4 boneless, skinless
chicken breasts

Salt

Freshly ground black pepper

4 Swiss cheese slices

4 cooked ham slices

1 cup Italian breadcrumbs

1 bunch thin asparagus
spears, trimmed

3 tablespoons extra-virgin
olive oil

1. Preheat the oven to 375°F. Spray the sheet pan with nonstick cooking spray.

2. Lay the chicken breasts on a cutting board, and cover each with a piece of plastic wrap. Use a mallet or a small, heavy frying pan to pound them to ¼ inch thick. Discard the plastic wrap, and sprinkle salt and pepper on both sides of the chicken.

3. Place 1 slice of Swiss cheese and 1 slice of ham on top of each chicken breast. Roll up each breast, securing each with a tooth-pick. Place on the sheet pan. Sprinkle the chicken rolls with the breadcrumbs, pressing so the crumbs stick to the chicken.

4. In a large bowl, toss the asparagus with the olive oil, and season with salt and pepper. Arrange the asparagus on the sheet pan around the chicken.

5. Bake for 30 minutes, or until the chicken is golden brown and just cooked through, and serve.

FROM THE FREEZER: To freeze the chicken (minus the asparagus), follow steps 2 and 3. Arrange the uncooked chicken rolls in a disposable baking pan, cover tightly, and seal in a freezer bag. Freeze for up to 1 month. To cook, defrost in the refrigerator overnight, remove the cover, and cook as in step 5.

PER SERVING Calories: 509; Total Fat: 25g; Saturated Fat: 8g;
Cholesterol: 114mg; Sodium: 1,045mg; Total Carbohydrates: 28g;
Sugars: 4g; Protein: 43g

Loaded Zucchini Boats

DAIRY-FREE • NUT-FREE

I love the simplicity of this old-fashioned comfort food—so refreshing, light, and full of flavor. Plus, these zucchini boats are healthy and super yummy. To give them even more flavor, use sweet or spicy bulk Italian sausage in place of the ground beef.

SERVES 4
PREP TIME: 10 MINUTES
COOK TIME: 30 MINUTES

Nonstick cooking spray

1 pound lean ground beef

½ cup jarred marinara sauce

½ cup diced onion

1 teaspoon freshly ground black pepper

4 medium zucchini, halved lengthwise

1 cup Italian breadcrumbs

Optional garnish:

1 teaspoon chopped fresh parsley

1. Preheat the oven to 400°F. Lightly coat the sheet pan with nonstick cooking spray.

2. In a large bowl, combine the ground beef, marinara sauce, onion, and pepper.

3. Using a teaspoon, remove the seedy core from a zucchini half. Lightly stuff the zucchini with some of the beef mixture, and top with breadcrumbs. Repeat with the rest of the zucchini.

4. Place the stuffed zucchini on the sheet pan. Bake for 30 minutes, or until the zucchini is tender. Garnish with the parsley, if using, and serve.

INGREDIENT TIP: When buying zucchini, always look for ones that are firm, with bright color and no blemishes. Unwashed zucchini can be stored in the refrigerator for up to 5 days.

PER SERVING Calories: 314; Total Fat: 10g; Saturated Fat: 3g; Cholesterol: 70mg; Sodium: 464mg; Total Carbohydrates: 29g; Sugars: 7g; Protein: 29g

One-Sheet Pork Chops

SHEET PAN · 10-INCH SKILLET

DAIRY-FREE · NUT-FREE

For a fun weeknight dinner, consider these pork chops with a side of Brussels sprouts. They are destined to be together, and this is a delicious way to get your kids to eat their veggies. Plus, the strong, spicy flavor from the Dijon mustard brings a whole new element to these chops.

SERVES 4
PREP TIME: 5 MINUTES
COOK TIME: 25 MINUTES

4 (8- to 10-ounce) pork chops, 1 inch thick

1 tablespoon Dijon mustard

1 cup Italian-style panko breadcrumbs

Nonstick cooking spray

Salt

Freshly ground black pepper

1 pound Brussels sprouts, trimmed and halved

2 tablespoons extra-virgin olive oil

1 teaspoon chopped fresh rosemary

1. Arrange a rack in the middle of the oven and preheat to 400°F. Place the sheet pan in the oven as it is heating.

2. Pat the pork chops dry with a paper towel, and set on a plate. Spread the Dijon mustard on both sides of the chops. Then sprinkle the breadcrumbs on both sides, pressing the crumbs into the mustard so they stick.

3. Remove the sheet pan from the oven and lightly coat with nonstick cooking spray. Place the pork chops on the sheet pan, and season with salt and pepper.

4. Put the Brussels sprouts in a large bowl. Coat them with the olive oil and season with the rosemary, salt, and pepper. Transfer the Brussels sprouts to the sheet pan, and arrange in a single layer around the perimeter of the pan.

5. Bake for 10 minutes. Flip the pork chops and Brussels sprouts. Continue cooking until the breadcrumbs are golden brown, 10 to 12 minutes.

6. To serve, place one crispy, crusted pork chop on each plate with a quarter of the Brussels sprouts.

COOKWARE SWAP: The pork chops can also be cooked in a 10-inch skillet. Prepare the chops as in step 2, season with salt and pepper, and place in a hot skillet over medium-high heat. Cook for 8 to 10 minutes on each side. You may need a larger skillet, depending on the size of your chops.

PER SERVING Calories: 351; Total Fat: 21g; Saturated Fat: 6g; Cholesterol: 55mg; Sodium: 587mg; Total Carbohydrates: 16g; Sugars: 3g; Protein: 30g

Baking Dish

A baking dish is a deep dish that can be put in the oven—and go straight to the dinner table (on a trivet, of course, so you don't burn your table). It is also called a casserole dish, although it's great for more than just casseroles. A baking dish can also be used for a slow oven braise, to roast chicken breasts, and for baked pasta dishes. The recipes in this book use a 4-quart rectangular baking dish that is about 14 by 10 by 2 inches. You can certainly use one with different dimensions, but it should be a 4-quart capacity.

While not all baking dishes are the same—they are made of different materials and come in varying sizes with different features—they are all suitable for most tasks. However, choosing the right materials for the dish can do wonders for the taste of your food. For example, you should not use a metal baking dish for making casseroles, since metal heats up very quickly.

Rustic Potato Galette, page 109

- **Use a ceramic or glass baking dish;** it warms up more slowly than metal, holds the heat once it's hot, and cooks the food evenly at a consistent temperature. Glass conducts heat extremely well and is fantastic for making casseroles and other dishes where browning is less important. It also has the advantage of being nonreactive, which means you can store food right in the baking dish without worrying that the food will pick up metallic flavors. Ceramic pans also conduct heat very well, but can cause your sweet dishes to overbrown.

- Know your oven, and be sure to **set it to the right temperature.** When you have a creamy dish, don't set your temperature too high. Start with 350°F, then increase it for the last 10 to 15 minutes, or use a broiler to get a crust on top.

- Once your dish is in the oven, give it some time to work its magic. Take a peek through the glass on your oven door, and **do not open the oven door** too often. You want the temperature inside the oven to stay the same.

- If your dish gets dark too quickly, **cover it with foil and lower the temperature.**

Squash Casserole

BAKING DISH

NUT-FREE · VEGETARIAN

Sweet squash and starchy potatoes make a nice base for this garlicky casserole, but it's possible that the most irresistible part of this dish is the crunchy, cheesy breadcrumb topping. It's especially addictive when you use the fresh thyme.

SERVES 4
PREP TIME: 5 MINUTES
COOK TIME: 30 MINUTES

Nonstick cooking spray

2 garlic cloves, finely minced

3 tablespoons extra-virgin olive oil

Salt

Freshly ground black pepper

3 medium yellow squash, sliced ¼ inch thick

3 Yukon gold potatoes, sliced ¼ inch thick

2 cups panko breadcrumbs

2 tablespoons grated Parmesan cheese

Optional garnish:

1 teaspoon finely chopped fresh thyme

1. Preheat the oven to 400°F. Spray the baking dish with nonstick cooking spray.

2. In a small bowl, combine the garlic and olive oil, and season with salt and pepper.

3. Arrange the squash and potato slices, overlapping one another, in the baking dish. Drizzle the oil mixture on top, and sprinkle with the breadcrumbs and Parmesan cheese.

4. Bake for 30 minutes, or until the potatoes are cooked through. Garnish with thyme, if using, and serve.

PREP TIP: This recipe can be prepared one day in advance. Follow steps 2 and 3, then cover the baking dish tightly with plastic wrap and refrigerate. When you're ready to bake, bring the dish to room temperature and continue with step 4.

PER SERVING Calories: 261; Total Fat: 12g; Saturated Fat: 2g; Cholesterol: 3mg; Sodium: 162mg; Total Carbohydrates: 35g; Sugars: 4g; Protein: 7g

Easy Veggie and Quinoa Casserole

BAKING DISH

FREEZER-FRIENDLY · GLUTEN-FREE · NUT-FREE · VEGETARIAN

This dish proves that eating healthy doesn't have to be boring. Quinoa is a nutritious grain-like food that's loaded with protein. It makes a great base for this casserole, which gets flavor from store-bought enchilada sauce, sweet corn kernels, and shredded cheese.

SERVES 4
PREP TIME: 5 MINUTES
COOK TIME: 25 MINUTES

Extra-virgin olive oil, for coating

1 cup quinoa

2 cups sliced bell peppers, mixed colors

1 (10-ounce) can mild enchilada sauce

½ cup corn kernels, frozen, canned, or roasted

1 cup shredded cheddar cheese

1½ cups water

Salt

Freshly ground black pepper

Optional garnish:

1 avocado, peeled, pitted, and diced

1 roma tomato, diced

1. Preheat the oven to 350°F. Coat the baking dish with olive oil.

2. In the baking dish, combine the quinoa, bell peppers, enchilada sauce, corn, cheese, and water, and season with salt and pepper. Stir gently to mix.

3. Cover with foil and bake for 20 minutes. Uncover, and bake for another 5 minutes, or until the cheese is bubbling.

4. Scatter the avocado and tomato on top, if using, and serve.

FROM THE FREEZER: To freeze this casserole, follow step 2, then tightly wrap in plastic wrap and slip into a large freezer bag. Freeze for up to 1 month. Thaw overnight in the refrigerator before proceeding with step 3.

PER SERVING Calories: 355; Total Fat: 16g; Saturated Fat: 7g; Cholesterol: 30mg; Sodium: 296mg; Total Carbohydrates: 39g; Sugars: 1g; Protein: 15g

 # Asparagus Tart

BAKING DISH

NUT-FREE • VEGETARIAN

During the dog days of summer, I often crave something light for dinner. This vegetable tart paired with a crisp green salad is the perfect solution. The tang of the mustard mixed with the asparagus and cheese makes an irresistible meal that you can enjoy for lunch or dinner.

SERVES 4
PREP TIME: 10 MINUTES
COOK TIME: 30 MINUTES

All-purpose flour, for dusting

1 sheet frozen puff pastry, thawed in the refrigerator

2 tablespoons honey Dijon mustard

2 cups shredded cheese, combination of fontina and Swiss, divided

1 pound asparagus, trimmed

1 tablespoon extra-virgin olive oil

Salt

Freshly ground black pepper

1. Preheat the oven to 400°F. Line the baking dish with parchment paper.

2. On a lightly floured surface, roll out the puff pastry into a 16-by-10-inch rectangle. Transfer to your lined baking dish, and trim the edges. Bake for 10 minutes, or until golden brown.

3. Brush the mustard over the puff pastry, and sprinkle 1 cup of cheese evenly over the top. Lay the asparagus over the cheese in a single layer, alternating the direction of the tips. Brush with the olive oil, and season with salt and pepper. Sprinkle with the remaining cup of cheese.

4. Bake for 20 minutes and serve.

INGREDIENT TIP: Puff pastry may sound intimidating, but it is a miracle ingredient because it puffs into light, flaky, buttery layers and makes your baking totally fancy. You can find puff pastry in the frozen-food aisle in supermarkets. Frozen puff pastry comes folded in a package and needs to be unfolded when you are ready to use it. Unfolding can cause the pastry to crack or break. If it does, wait a few minutes and try again. But don't leave it at room temperature for too long because it can get sticky. If the pastry sheet gets too soft, return it to the refrigerator for 20 to 30 minutes before continuing.

PER SERVING Calories: 763; Total Fat: 55g; Saturated Fat: 21g; Cholesterol: 59mg; Sodium: 611mg; Total Carbohydrates: 46g; Sugars: 5g; Protein: 2g

Baked Tater Tots Casserole

BAKING DISH

FREEZER-FRIENDLY · NUT-FREE · VEGETARIAN

You may be laughing now, but you know as well as I do that if this were put in front of you, you would happily munch it right up. Creamy mushroom soup and cheese are exactly what tater tots have been waiting for all this time. Peas and carrots help you justify this as a meal and not just an indulgent snack.

SERVES 4
PREP TIME: 5 MINUTES
COOK TIME: 20 MINUTES

1 (10¾-ounce) can condensed cream of mushroom soup

2 cups frozen mixed carrots and peas

3 cups frozen tater tots

2 cups shredded cheddar cheese

1 tablespoon chopped fresh parsley

1. Preheat the oven to 425°F.

2. In the baking dish, mix the cream of mushroom soup and carrots and peas, then spread evenly in the bottom. Lay the tater tots evenly on top, and top with the cheese.

3. Bake for 20 minutes, or until the tater tots are golden brown. Sprinkle with the parsley and serve.

FROM THE FREEZER: To freeze this casserole, follow step 2, then tightly wrap the dish in plastic wrap and slip it into a large freezer bag. Freeze for up to 1 month. When you're ready to bake, remove the wrap, place directly into an oven preheated to 350°F, and bake for about 20 minutes or until heated through.

PER SERVING Calories: 491; Total Fat: 31g; Saturated Fat: 15g; Cholesterol: 59mg; Sodium: 1,288mg; Total Carbohydrates: 30g; Sugars: 3g; Protein: 18g

Rustic Potato Galette

GLUTEN-FREE · NUT-FREE · VEGETARIAN

You can have your potato cake and eat it, too. And in just 30 minutes! This dish is a simple mix of potatoes and cheese complemented beautifully by shallots and rosemary, which round out the flavor. It will have everyone coming back for seconds.

SERVES 3 to 4
PREP TIME: 5 MINUTES
COOK TIME: 30 MINUTES

2 tablespoons extra-virgin olive oil, plus more for coating

1 pound Yukon gold potatoes, scrubbed, cut into ⅛-inch-thick slices

½ cup grated Gruyère cheese

2 shallots, finely chopped

1 teaspoon minced fresh rosemary

Salt

Freshly ground black pepper

3 tablespoons grated Parmesan cheese

1. Preheat the oven to 450°F. Brush the baking dish with a little olive oil.

2. In a large bowl, combine the potatoes, Gruyère cheese, shallots, rosemary, and olive oil, and season with salt and pepper.

3. Arrange half of the potatoes inside the dish in concentric circles, overlapping the slices slightly. Sprinkle with about half of the Parmesan cheese. Repeat the process once more with the remaining potatoes and Parmesan.

4. Roast for 30 minutes, or until the top is golden and the potatoes are tender, and serve.

VARIATION: Swiss cheese will work nicely in this dish in place of Gruyère.

PER SERVING Calories: 295; Total Fat: 17g; Saturated Fat: 6g; Cholesterol: 26mg; Sodium: 208mg; Total Carbohydrates: 26g; Sugars: 2g; Protein: 11g

Super Cheesy Lasagna

BAKING DISH

FREEZER-FRIENDLY · NUT-FREE · VEGETARIAN

Using no-boil noodles and store-bought sauce makes it both quick and easy to create a luscious pan of cheesy lasagna. It's a bonus that you can also load it up with spinach as a sneaky way to get your kids to eat their greens.

SERVES 8
PREP TIME: 5 MINUTES
COOK TIME: 25 MINUTES

Extra-virgin olive oil,
for coating

2 (10-ounce) packages frozen chopped spinach, thawed

1 (15-ounce) container ricotta cheese

Salt

Freshly ground black pepper

1 (24-ounce) jar marinara sauce with basil, divided

8 ounces dried no-boil lasagna noodles, divided

3 cups shredded mozzarella cheese, divided

1. Preheat the oven to 425°F. Coat the baking dish with a little olive oil.

2. Squeeze the spinach to remove as much liquid as possible. In a large bowl, combine the spinach with the ricotta, and season with salt and pepper. Mix well.

3. Spread ½ cup of marinara sauce in the bottom of the baking dish. Arrange 3 or 4 lasagna noodles to cover it. Spread a third of the ricotta mixture over the noodles, followed by ½ cup of marinara sauce. Sprinkle with 1 cup of mozzarella cheese. Repeat to make two more layers, ending with mozzarella cheese on top.

4. Bake uncovered for 25 minutes, or until brown and bubbling, and serve.

FROM THE FREEZER: To freeze this lasagna, assemble it as in steps 2 and 3. Cover tightly with plastic wrap, and seal in a freezer bag. Freeze for up to 1 month. To cook, defrost in the refrigerator overnight, remove the cover, and cook as in step 4.

PER SERVING Calories: 312; Total Fat: 12g; Saturated Fat: 5g; Cholesterol: 29mg; Sodium: 457mg; Total Carbohydrates: 36g; Sugars: 6g; Protein: 16g

Ravioli and Spinach Bake

NUT-FREE • VEGETARIAN

Using frozen ravioli in place of lasagna noodles is nothing short of genius. You can pick any type of ravioli you like (filled with mushrooms, cheese, spinach, sausage, or whatever you like), and all you have to do is layer it in a baking dish with a jar of marinara sauce, some fresh spinach, and shredded cheese.

SERVES 4
PREP TIME: 5 MINUTES
COOK TIME: 30 MINUTES

Nonstick cooking spray

1 (24-ounce) jar
marinara sauce

3 cups baby spinach

2 (30-ounce) packages frozen
cheese ravioli

1½ cups shredded
mozzarella cheese

2 tablespoons chopped
fresh basil

1. Preheat the oven to 400°F. Spray a baking dish with nonstick cooking spray.

2. Spread half the sauce in the bottom of the baking dish. Add half the baby spinach, then evenly spread 1 package of ravioli over the spinach. Sprinkle with half the mozzarella cheese. Repeat the process once again, topping with mozzarella.

3. Bake for 30 minutes. Garnish with the basil leaves and serve.

PREP TIP: This recipe can be prepared one day in advance. Simply follow step 2, then cover tightly with plastic wrap and refrigerate. When you're ready to bake, bring to room temperature and continue with step 3.

PER SERVING Calories: 926; Total Fat: 26g; Saturated Fat: 15g; Cholesterol: 181mg; Sodium: 1682mg; Total Carbohydrates: 128g; Sugars: 13g; Protein: 44g

Roasted Vegetable Frittata

BAKING DISH • 10-INCH SKILLET

GLUTEN-FREE • NUT-FREE • VEGETARIAN

Frittata is a great dish either for quick meals or to make ahead and keep on hand for those days when you have no time at all to cook. The preparation is simple, and a handful of flavorful ingredients, like garlic and cheese, make it shine.

SERVES 4 to 6
PREP TIME: 5 MINUTES
COOK TIME: 25 MINUTES

Nonstick cooking spray

3 cups diced mixed white potato, sweet potato, and zucchini

2 garlic cloves, finely minced

1 tablespoon fresh thyme

1 tablespoon extra-virgin olive oil

Salt

Freshly ground black pepper

6 eggs, whisked

1 cup grated Parmesan cheese

1. Preheat the oven to 425°F. Spray the baking dish with nonstick cooking spray.

2. Put the diced mixed veggies, garlic, and thyme in the baking dish. Add the olive oil, season with salt and pepper, and toss well. Bake uncovered for 15 minutes.

3. Pour in the eggs, and sprinkle with the cheese. Cover with a piece of aluminum foil, bake for another 10 minutes, and serve.

COOKWARE SWAP: This recipe can also be cooked in a 10-inch skillet. Heat the oil, then add the diced veggies, garlic, and thyme. Cover the skillet and cook over medium-low heat for 10 to 15 minutes, or until the potatoes are just tender. Uncover and increase the heat to medium-high. Continue cooking for another 8 to 10 minutes, turning occasionally, until the potatoes are golden brown. Pour in the eggs, season with salt and pepper, then sprinkle the Parmesan cheese over the top. Cover and cook until the egg is lightly browned on the bottom, 3 to 5 minutes. Carefully flip the frittata and cook until the bottom is lightly browned, 2 to 3 minutes more.

PER SERVING Calories: 263; Total Fat: 16g; Saturated Fat: 7g; Cholesterol: 266mg; Sodium: 395mg; Total Carbohydrates: 12g; Sugars: 1g; Protein: 19g

Broccoli-Cheddar Quiche

BAKING DISH

FREEZER-FRIENDLY · NUT-FREE · VEGETARIAN

Eggs form the basis for some of the best any-time-of-day meals. Quiche is one of my favorite ways to serve them. Using frozen pie crust makes this recipe easier to accomplish than making scrambled eggs. Plus, the combination of broccoli and cheddar cheese is always a winner.

SERVES 4
PREP TIME: 5 MINUTES
COOK TIME: 30 MINUTES

4 eggs

1 cup milk

1½ cups shredded cheddar cheese, divided

Salt

Freshly ground black pepper

4 cups (1 pound) frozen broccoli florets

1 (9-inch) premade piecrust in a tin

1. Preheat the oven to 375°F.

2. In a large bowl, combine the eggs, milk, and half the cheese, and season with salt and pepper. Mix well.

3. Spread the broccoli in the pie crust. Pour in the egg mixture. Sprinkle the rest of the cheese over the top.

4. Bake for 30 minutes and serve.

FROM THE FREEZER: To freeze this quiche, follow steps 2 through 4. Cool the casserole, then tightly wrap in plastic wrap and slip into a large freezer bag. Freeze for up to 1 month. When you're ready to serve it, remove the wrap, place directly into an oven preheated to 350°F, and bake for about 20 minutes or until heated through.

PER SERVING Calories: 447; Total Fat: 30g; Saturated Fat: 13g; Cholesterol: 213mg; Sodium: 717mg; Total Carbohydrates: 23g; Sugars: 6g; Protein: 21g

Honey-Mustard Chicken

BAKING DISH

DAIRY-FREE · GLUTEN-FREE · NUT-FREE

Honey-mustard chicken is a favorite in many homes—including mine—for good reason. It's as simple as combining equal parts honey and Dijon mustard, tossing it with strips of chicken and potato wedges, and baking it in the oven. The savory-sweet flavor is perfectly addictive.

SERVES 4
PREP TIME: 5 MINUTES
COOK TIME: 30 MINUTES

1 pound large Yukon gold potatoes, cut into wedges

2 tablespoons extra-virgin olive oil

Salt

Freshly ground black pepper

4 to 6 boneless, skinless chicken breasts, cut into strips

½ cup Dijon mustard

½ cup honey

1 teaspoon paprika

Optional garnish:

Juice of 1 lemon

1. Preheat the oven to 400°F.

2. Arrange the potatoes in the baking dish. Add the olive oil, and season with salt and pepper. Lay the chicken strips on top of the potatoes.

3. In a small bowl, combine the mustard, honey, and paprika. Pour the mixture over the chicken.

4. Bake for 30 minutes. Sprinkle with lemon juice, if using, just before serving.

PREP TIP: The smaller you cut the potatoes, the faster they will bake. Leave the skin on to minimize prep time.

PER SERVING Calories: 819; Total Fat: 20g; Saturated Fat: 2g; Cholesterol: 130mg; Sodium: 954mg; Total Carbohydrates: 109g; Sugars: 73g; Protein: 59g

Chicken and Brussels Sprouts Casserole

BAKING DISH

GLUTEN-FREE · NUT-FREE

Even devoted Brussels sprouts naysayers have been converted with this dish. The creamy cheese sauce counterbalances any bitterness from the veggies. Boneless, skinless chicken breast makes it a meal.

SERVES 4
PREP TIME: 5 MINUTES
COOK TIME: 30 MINUTES

Nonstick cooking spray

2 cups half-and-half

1 cup milk

2 cups shredded Swiss cheese, divided

Salt

Freshly ground black pepper

1 pound Brussels sprouts, trimmed and halved

2 tablespoons extra-virgin olive oil

4 boneless, skinless chicken breasts, cut into bite-size pieces

1. Preheat the oven to 400°F. Spray the baking dish with nonstick cooking spray.

2. In a large bowl, combine the half-and-half, milk, and 1 cup of cheese, and season with salt and pepper.

3. Arrange the Brussels sprouts in the bottom of the baking dish. Add the oil, and season with salt and pepper.

4. Arrange the chicken on top of the Brussels sprouts. Pour the milk mixture over the chicken, and top with the remaining cup of cheese.

5. Bake for 30 minutes, until the chicken is cooked and the cheese is bubbly, and serve.

INGREDIENT TIP: When shopping for Brussels sprouts, look for tightly packed, bright green sprouts that are firm and heavy.

PER SERVING Calories: 623; Total Fat: 39g; Saturated Fat: 20g; Cholesterol: 164mg; Sodium: 324mg; Total Carbohydrates: 21g; Sugars: 6g; Protein: 50g

Chicken Pot Pie

FREEZER-FRIENDLY · **NUT-FREE**

Talk about a dish that's labor-intensive to make from scratch, but boy is it worth it. Chicken pot pies are the very definition of comfort food. This version takes a few shortcuts—using precooked chicken (either leftovers or a rotisserie chicken from the supermarket will do), canned cream of chicken soup, and frozen puff pastry—to make this meal a cinch without sacrificing any of that comforting goodness.

SERVES 4
PREP TIME: 5 MINUTES
COOK TIME: 30 MINUTES

Nonstick cooking spray

1 cup diced cooked chicken

1 cup frozen mirepoix

1 (10¾-ounce) can condensed cream of chicken soup

All-purpose flour, for dusting

1 sheet frozen puff pastry, thawed in the refrigerator

1 egg, whisked

1. Preheat the oven to 400°F. Spray the baking dish with nonstick cooking spray.

2. In the baking dish, combine the chicken, mirepoix, and cream of chicken soup, mixing well.

3. Unfold the puff pastry, and gently roll it out on a lightly floured board so it is large enough to cover the baking dish. Set it over the top, and trim the extra pastry all around.

4. Brush the top with the egg, and make 2 or 3 slits in the pastry with a sharp knife. Bake for 30 minutes and serve.

FROM THE FREEZER: To freeze this chicken pot pie, assemble it as in steps 2 and 3. Then tightly wrap it in plastic wrap and slip into a freezer bag. Freeze for up to 2 months. When you're ready, brush the top with egg and make 2 or 3 slits in the pastry. Place directly in the oven and bake at 400°F for 50 minutes, or until the edges turn brown.

PER SERVING Calories: 233; Total Fat: 11g; Saturated Fat: 3g; Cholesterol: 74mg; Sodium: 582mg; Total Carbohydrates: 17g; Sugars: 2g; Protein: 16g

Turkey and Biscuit Bake

NUT-FREE

This is my favorite recipe for using leftover turkey. The sweetness from the buttermilk biscuits pairs perfectly with the cream of chicken soup to create something truly special. And it definitely tastes like dinner at Grandma's, but without all the hard work. Your family will gobble this up.

SERVES 4
PREP TIME: 10 MINUTES
COOK TIME: 30 MINUTES

Nonstick cooking spray

1 (10¾-ounce) can condensed cream of chicken soup

¼ cup milk

2 cups diced cooked turkey

1 cup frozen mixed peas and carrots

1 (12-ounce) tube refrigerated buttermilk biscuits

1. Preheat the oven to 400°F. Spray the baking dish with nonstick cooking spray.

2. Add the chicken soup and milk to the baking dish, and stir gently. Add the turkey and peas and carrots, then top with the biscuits, placing them close together so they will form a crust on top as they bake and expand.

3. Bake for 30 minutes, or until the biscuits are golden brown, and serve.

VARIATION: You can substitute cooked chicken for the turkey.

PER SERVING Calories: 472; Total Fat: 20g; Saturated Fat: 5g; Cholesterol: 60mg; Sodium: 1,510mg; Total Carbohydrates: 44g; Sugars: 7g; Protein: 28g

Southwestern Casserole

GLUTEN-FREE · NUT-FREE

What could be better on a winter's night than a cheesy, spicy casserole with a delicious Italian sausage twist? This potato-based casserole hits all the right notes. Black beans give it protein and fiber, and sausage brings more protein and tons of flavor. Tomatoes, cheese, and jalapeño give it richness, tanginess, and a little kick of heat.

SERVES 4
PREP TIME: 5 MINUTES
COOK TIME: 30 MINUTES

Nonstick cooking spray

2 cups diced Yukon gold potatoes

2 Italian sausages, casings removed

2 (14½-ounce) cans diced tomatoes

1 (16-ounce) can black beans, rinsed and drained

2 cups shredded Monterey Jack cheese

Optional garnish:

2 jalapeños, seeded and chopped

1. Preheat the oven to 400°F. Spray the baking dish with nonstick cooking spray.

2. Arrange the potatoes in the baking dish. In a large bowl, mix together the sausages, tomatoes with their juices, and black beans, and add to the baking dish. Top with the cheese.

3. Cover with aluminum foil and bake for 25 minutes.

4. Uncover and broil for 5 minutes, or until bubbling and heated through, and serve.

PREP TIP: To remove sausage casings easily, cut the sausage lengthwise with a sharp knife, then scrape or squeeze out the meat.

PER SERVING Calories: 692; Total Fat: 34g; Saturated Fat: 16g; Cholesterol: 85mg; Sodium: 687mg; Total Carbohydrates: 67g; Sugars: 26g; Protein: 38g

Sausage Pizza Casserole

FREEZER-FRIENDLY · NUT-FREE

Everyone loves pizza, right? Just wait until you try this pizza pie casserole—*love* is not a strong enough word. Sweet bell peppers and spicy Italian sausage come together to create a delicious casserole with all of your favorite pizza flavors. Plus it's topped with cheesy goodness. How can you beat it?

SERVES 4
PREP TIME: 5 MINUTES
COOK TIME: 30 MINUTES

Nonstick cooking spray

1 (16-ounce) package refrigerated pizza dough

1 (15-ounce) jar marinara sauce

4 mild Italian sausages (about 8 ounces), casings removed

2 cups sliced bell peppers, mixed colors

3 cups shredded provolone cheese

Optional garnish:

1 teaspoon red pepper flakes

1. Preheat the oven to 350°F. Lightly coat the baking dish with nonstick cooking spray.

2. Line the baking dish with the pizza dough. Spoon the marinara sauce evenly onto the dough. Layer with the sausage meat, bell peppers, and cheese.

3. Bake for 30 minutes, or until the crust is light golden brown at the edges.

4. Sprinkle with the red pepper flakes, if using, and serve.

FROM THE FREEZER: To freeze this casserole, assemble it as in step 2. Then tightly wrap in plastic and slip into a freezer bag. Freeze for up to 1 month. Thaw overnight in the refrigerator before proceeding with steps 3 and 4.

PER SERVING Calories: 743; Total Fat: 45g; Saturated Fat: 22g; Cholesterol: 109mg; Sodium: 2,142mg; Total Carbohydrates: 48g; Sugars: 8g; Protein: 42g

Roasting Pan 7

A roasting pan is not something to pull out once a year when Thanksgiving rolls around. There are so many more uses for this cookware staple than just roasting a turkey. You can also roast chicken, lamb, and vegetables, and it's great for one-pot dinners when you're cooking for the whole family. It can also work as a casserole dish for big batches of lasagna or enchiladas.

Roasting an entire meal in one pan is an easy way to feed your family on a weeknight or on a busy weekend when errands have consumed most of the day. Just plop the meat and vegetables, along with some seasonings and maybe a sauce, into a roasting pan, put it in the oven, and in about an hour or so (time you can be doing something else), depending on how long it takes to cook the meat, you'll have a complete dinner ready for four to six people. Once you get the hang of roasting your dinner, you can vary the recipes in this book any way you'd like.

The ideal roasting plan should have sides that are 2 to 3 inches high, which ensures that the meat and juices are contained in the pan, while the heat easily circulates. This means your meat will brown and crisp perfectly. Some roasting pans have straight sides, while others have sides that flare out; both pans work equally well. It is great to have at least two roasting pans: a small, 9-by-13-inch pan and a medium, 10-by-14-inch pan.

Roasted Chicken with Thai Mango Salad, page 134

When it comes to roasting, you can have all of the right ingredients on hand for the perfect recipe, but if you don't have the right roasting pan, your finished product might end up burnt and stuck to the bottom. So here are some things to keep in mind.

- **Invest in a good roasting pan**. A good option is a heavy-duty stainless steel pan with no nonstick coating. Nonstick coatings aren't the best choice when you're cooking with high heat, because they don't hold up. Stainless steel pans cost a bit more, but they are durable, clean up easily, and will last a lifetime if you look after them well.

- **Pair foods with similar cooking times.** Meats that cook quickly, like fish and chicken breasts, should be paired with delicate vegetables like mushrooms, bell peppers, and yellow squash. Meats that take more cooking time, like beef roasts, chops, and whole birds, can be roasted along with potatoes, carrots, and other root vegetables.

- To make cook time even faster, **cut vegetables into equal, midsize pieces.** Smaller pieces cook faster, but they have more potential to burn, while larger pieces don't always cook through.

- **Don't overcrowd the pan,** or you will end up with soggy vegetables.

Roasted Bell Pepper Salad

9-BY-13-INCH ROASTING PAN · BAKING SHEET

EXTRA-QUICK · DAIRY-FREE · GLUTEN-FREE · NUT-FREE · VEGAN

Get your daily dose of veggies with this simple roasted and raw vegetable salad. The sweetness of the balsamic vinegar cuts any bitterness from the peppers. Capers add a burst of salty, briny goodness that heightens all the other flavors in this dish.

SERVES 4
PREP TIME: 10 MINUTES
COOK TIME: 10 MINUTES

6 large bell peppers, mixed colors

1 English cucumber

2 tablespoons extra-virgin olive oil

½ teaspoon balsamic vinegar

Salt

Freshly ground black pepper

1 tablespoon capers, rinsed and drained

2 tablespoons chopped fresh basil

1. Preheat the broiler. Line the roasting pan with aluminum foil, for easier cleanup later.

2. Place the whole bell peppers in the roasting pan. Place on the top rack and broil, turning occasionally, for 8 to 10 minutes. The skin will blister and turn black.

3. Remove the peppers and cool completely in a large bowl covered with plastic wrap. Then seed the peppers and cut the flesh into strips. Halve the cucumber lengthwise, then chop up both halves.

4. In a small bowl, whisk together the olive oil and vinegar, and season with salt and pepper.

5. Divide the peppers evenly among four plates. Scatter the cucumber, capers, and basil around the peppers. Drizzle the dressing over everything and serve.

COOKWARE SWAP: This recipe can also be made on a baking sheet. You don't have to change a thing!

PER SERVING Calories: 129; Total Fat: 8g; Saturated Fat: 1g; Cholesterol: 0mg; Sodium: 109mg; Total Carbohydrates: 16g; Sugars: 10g; Protein: 2g

 # Roasted Corn Salad

9-BY-13-INCH ROASTING PAN

DAIRY-FREE · GLUTEN-FREE · NUT-FREE · VEGAN

What would a summer salad be without corn on the cob? This roasted corn salad is so fresh it will make you weak in the knees. It's a fantastic accompaniment to anything grilled—steak, fish, sausages, or even lobster or other shellfish.

SERVES 4
PREP TIME: 10 MINUTES
COOK TIME: 20 MINUTES

Nonstick cooking spray

8 ears corn

2 tablespoons extra-virgin olive oil, divided

1 (5-ounce) package baby spinach

¼ cup diced red onion

2 plum tomatoes, diced

¼ cup freshly squeezed lime juice

Salt

Freshly ground black pepper

Optional garnish:

¼ cup chopped fresh cilantro

1. Preheat the oven to 400°F. Coat the roasting pan with non-stick cooking spray.

2. Brush the corn with 1 tablespoon of olive oil, and place it in the prepared pan. Roast for 20 minutes, or until the corn is golden brown and tender.

3. Cut the kernels from the cobs and transfer to a bowl. Add the baby spinach, red onion, tomatoes, lime juice, and the remaining 1 tablespoon of olive oil. Season with salt and pepper. Sprinkle with the cilantro, if using, and serve.

VARIATION: To make this dish with frozen corn kernels, put 1 cup of corn in a colander or strainer under cold running water until thawed, and drain thoroughly. Toss with oil, spread out in the baking pan, and roast as in step 2.

PER SERVING Calories: 215; Total Fat: 9g; Saturated Fat: 1g; Cholesterol: 0mg; Sodium: 97mg; Total Carbohydrates: 34g; Sugars: 8g; Protein: 7g

Roasted Eggplant Pitas

9-BY-13-INCH ROASTING PAN

EXTRA-QUICK · NUT-FREE · VEGETARIAN

Roasting eggplant is kitchen magic at its best. High heat turns this tricky vegetable from spongy and slightly bitter to silky and sweet. Creamy Greek yogurt, tart lemon, slices of red onion, and even fresh mint leaves, if you like, give this sandwich a full complement of textures and flavors.

SERVES 4
PREP TIME: 10 MINUTES
COOK TIME: 10 MINUTES

2 medium purple eggplants, sliced

2 tablespoons extra-virgin olive oil

Salt

Freshly ground black pepper

¼ cup plain Greek yogurt

Juice of ½ lemon

3 whole-wheat pita rounds, halved

1 small red onion, thinly sliced

Optional garnish:

¼ cup torn fresh mint leaves

1. Preheat the oven to 400°F, and place the rack 4 to 6 inches from the broiler. Line the roasting pan with aluminum foil for quick cleanup later.

2. Place the eggplant slices in the pan. Brush both sides with the olive oil, and season with salt and pepper. Broil for 4 minutes on each side, until the eggplant looks collapsed and puckered.

3. In a small bowl, combine the yogurt and lemon juice, and season with salt and pepper. Fill each pita half evenly with the yogurt mixture, eggplant, onion, and mint leaves, if using, and serve.

VARIATION: For extra crunch, I like adding finely chopped iceberg lettuce to each pita.

PER SERVING Calories: 278; Total Fat: 9g; Saturated Fat: 1g; Cholesterol: 1mg; Sodium: 311mg; Total Carbohydrates: 45g; Sugars: 11g; Protein: 9g

Roasted Artichokes with Quinoa

9-BY-13-INCH ROASTING PAN

DAIRY-FREE · GLUTEN-FREE · NUT-FREE · VEGAN

I'd never thought of roasting artichoke hearts before creating this dish. Whatever was I thinking? Roasting them intensifies their seductive, earthy flavor. A quick toss in a combination of tart lemon juice and spicy red pepper flakes makes them addictive.

SERVES 4
PREP TIME: 10 MINUTES
COOK TIME: 20 MINUTES

4 (9-ounce) packages frozen artichoke hearts, thawed

3 tablespoons extra-virgin olive oil, divided

Salt

Freshly ground black pepper

1 cup quinoa

1¼ cups hot water

Juice of 1 lemon

1 teaspoon red pepper flakes

½ cup chopped fresh parsley

1. Preheat the oven to 350°F.

2. Arrange the artichoke hearts in the roasting pan. Toss with 2 tablespoons of olive oil, and season generously with salt and pepper. Roast for 20 minutes.

3. While they are roasting, in a large bowl, toss the quinoa with the remaining 1 tablespoon of olive oil. Pour the hot water over the quinoa, stir well, cover, and leave to stand for 10 to 15 minutes. Separate the grains with a fork, then season generously with salt and pepper.

4. Add the cooked artichoke hearts, lemon juice, red pepper flakes, and parsley to the bowl with the quinoa. Toss well to combine, and serve.

VARIATION: You can use couscous instead of quinoa. However, quinoa has a lot more protein and fiber—similar to beans. Couscous, meanwhile, is a simple carb, similar to white pasta.

PER SERVING Calories: 369; Total Fat: 14g; Saturated Fat: 2g; Cholesterol: 0mg; Sodium: 285mg; Total Carbohydrates: 55g; Sugars: 3g; Protein: 15g

 # Easy Roasted Salmon

10-BY-14-INCH ROASTING PAN

DAIRY-FREE · GLUTEN-FREE · NUT-FREE

Salmon is a firm favorite among seafood lovers. This dish does the fish justice, and it will quickly become a family favorite. Mustard and lemon together really enhance the elegant flavors of the salmon.

SERVES 4 to 6
PREP TIME: 5 MINUTES
COOK TIME: 35 MINUTES

1 pound small red potatoes, halved

4 tablespoons extra-virgin olive oil, divided

Salt

Freshly ground black pepper

¼ cup whole-grain mustard

¼ cup minced fresh chives

4 (6-ounce) skinless salmon fillets

1 lemon, cut into wedges

1. Preheat the oven to 500°F. Place the rack at the lowest level.

2. Place the potatoes on one side of the roasting pan, sprinkle with 2 tablespoons of olive oil, and season with salt and pepper. Roast for 15 minutes, flip with a spatula to ensure even browning, then continue roasting for another 10 minutes.

3. While the potatoes are cooking, in a small bowl, combine the remaining 2 tablespoons of olive oil with the mustard and chives. Pat the salmon dry with paper towels, then season generously with salt and pepper.

4. Lower the oven to 400°F. Place the salmon on the other side of the roasting pan, and spread the mustard mixture over it. Roast for 10 minutes, or until beginning to flake but slightly translucent at the center when checked with the tip of a paring knife.

5. Transfer to plates and serve with the lemon wedges.

VARIATION: When you're tired of white potatoes, try this recipe with sweet potatoes instead. Peel and halve them before cooking.

PER SERVING Calories: 547; Total Fat: 35g; Saturated Fat: 6g; Cholesterol: 97mg; Sodium: 144mg; Total Carbohydrates: 22g; Sugars: 2g; Protein: 38g

Miso-Glazed Salmon with Asparagus

EXTRA-QUICK · DAIRY-FREE · NUT-FREE

Miso is fermented soybean paste used in Japanese cooking, including the popular miso soup. Though it may look similar to hummus, miso is not meant to be eaten plain out of the container. When shopping for miso, you may find it called miso paste or soybean paste. It's usually in white plastic tubs near the refrigerated tofu, dairy substitutes, or international foods section. Mirin is Japanese rice wine, a staple in Japanese cooking that pairs well with soy sauce. It tastes a little like sake but is sweeter and has a lower alcohol content. You can find it in the international aisle or with the vinegar and cooking wine. If your store does not carry mirin, you can replace it with 2 tablespoons of sweet Marsala wine or dry white wine and 1 teaspoon of sugar.

SERVES 4
PREP TIME: 5 MINUTES
COOK TIME: 15 MINUTES

Nonstick cooking spray

2 tablespoons white miso paste

2 tablespoons mirin

1 tablespoon soy sauce

4 (6-ounce) skin-on salmon fillets

1 bunch asparagus, trimmed

2 tablespoons extra-virgin olive oil

Salt

Freshly ground black pepper

Optional garnish:

Sesame seeds

Thinly sliced scallion

1. Preheat the oven to 400°F. Position the rack 3 to 4 inches from the broiler. Line the roasting pan with aluminum foil, and spray with nonstick cooking spray.

2. In a small bowl, combine the miso paste, mirin, and soy sauce. Place the salmon, skin-side down, in the pan. Brush the miso paste generously over both sides of the salmon. Arrange the asparagus in the pan. Drizzle with the olive oil, and season with salt and pepper.

3. Broil for 5 to 8 minutes. When the fillets feel firm to the touch, flip them over and broil for another 2 minutes, or until cooked through and opaque in the center. Set aside. Continue roasting the asparagus for another 5 minutes, depending on the thickness, or until just tender, and serve with the salmon.

INGREDIENT TIP: Once the miso is opened, place a piece of parchment paper onto the top surface of the miso under the lid; then store in an airtight container in the refrigerator, and it will be good for 9 months to a year. But always pay attention to the best-by dates.

PER SERVING Calories: 417; Total Fat: 26g; Saturated Fat: 5g; Cholesterol: 103mg; Sodium: 829mg; Total Carbohydrates: 10g; Sugars: 4g; Protein: 37g

Tuna Steak with Cannellini

9-BY-13-INCH ROASTING PAN

EXTRA-QUICK · DAIRY-FREE · GLUTEN-FREE · NUT-FREE

A beautiful tuna steak doesn't need much to become an impressive dinner. Here, sweet tomatoes, creamy white beans, and sweet-tangy balsamic vinegar mingle to highlight the inherent wow factor of the meaty fish. Serve it with a green salad and a glass of crisp white wine.

SERVES 4
PREP TIME: 5 MINUTES
COOK TIME: 15 MINUTES

Nonstick cooking spray

4 (5-ounce) tuna steaks

Salt

Freshly ground black pepper

10 cups chopped romaine lettuce leaves (about 1½ heads)

1 cup canned cannellini (small white) beans, rinsed and drained

2 large vine-ripened tomatoes, cut into wedges

½ cup balsamic vinegar

1. Preheat the oven to 400°F. Lightly spray the roasting pan with nonstick cooking spray.

2. Season the tuna with salt and pepper. Roast in the pan for 15 minutes, or until the tuna is fork-tender.

3. Divide the lettuce among four plates. Top with equal amounts of white beans and tomato, then place a tuna steak on top. Drizzle with the balsamic vinegar and serve.

VARIATION: You can also cook swordfish steaks this way.

PER SERVING Calories: 234; Total Fat: 2g; Saturated Fat: 0g; Cholesterol: 56mg; Sodium: 198mg; Total Carbohydrates: 16g; Sugars: 4g; Protein: 39g

Garlic-Parmesan Roasted Shrimp

10-BY-14-INCH ROASTING PAN

GLUTEN-FREE · NUT-FREE

Shrimp is one of my favorite proteins to keep in the freezer because it's easy to defrost and cooks quickly. The plump, sweet flesh takes to just about any flavor profile you can think of, too. Here, garlic, Parmesan cheese, and oregano give it classic Italian flavor—and it takes just 30 minutes to prep and cook.

SERVES 4
PREP TIME: 5 MINUTES
COOK TIME: 25 MINUTES

Nonstick cooking spray

1 pound small red potatoes, halved

4 tablespoons extra-virgin olive oil, divided

Salt

Freshly ground black pepper

2 garlic cloves, minced

½ teaspoon dried oregano

½ cup grated Parmesan cheese

2 pounds shell-on extra-large shrimp

Optional garnish:

1 tablespoon chopped fresh parsley

1 lemon, cut into wedges

1. Preheat the oven to 450°F. Coat the roasting pan with non-stick cooking spray.

2. In the pan, toss the potatoes with 2 tablespoons of olive oil, and season with salt and pepper. Roast for 15 minutes, then flip with a spatula to ensure even browning.

3. In a small bowl, combine the remaining 2 tablespoons of olive oil and the garlic, oregano, and Parmesan cheese, and season with salt and pepper. Add the shrimp to the roasting pan, and toss with the olive oil mixture. Roast for 5 minutes. Flip and roast for another 5 minutes, or until the shrimp is pink, firm, and cooked through.

4. Leave it to cool slightly, then garnish with parsley and lemon wedges, if using, and serve.

FROM THE FREEZER: Plan ahead. Peel garlic cloves and store them in an airtight container in the freezer for 6 to 8 months. To thaw, simply run under hot water. Garlic is a low-acid food, which has a risk of bacterial growth at room temperature, so use it immediately after thawing.

PER SERVING Calories: 435; Total Fat: 17g; Saturated Fat: 4g; Cholesterol: 492mg; Sodium: 390mg; Total Carbohydrates: 19g; Sugars: 1g; Protein: 52g

Garlicky Roasted Chicken

9-BY-13-INCH ROASTING PAN

DAIRY-FREE · GLUTEN-FREE · NUT-FREE

This is the kind of meal every family should gather around once in a while. The flavors of garlic, rosemary, and chicken bring back memories of Sunday roast dinners cooked by mom—a very welcome meal in my home. I bet it's about to become a favorite in yours, too.

SERVES 8
PREP TIME: 5 MINUTES
COOK TIME: 25 MINUTES

2 tablespoons extra-virgin olive oil, plus more for coating the pan

2 pounds green beans, trimmed

Salt

Freshly ground black pepper

4 to 6 boneless, skin-on chicken breasts

10 garlic cloves, unpeeled

2 fresh rosemary sprigs

1. Preheat the oven to 425°F. Coat the roasting pan with olive oil.

2. In the roasting pan, toss the green beans with the olive oil, and season generously with salt and pepper.

3. Season the chicken with salt and pepper, then place in the roasting pan, skin-side down. Place the garlic and rosemary around the chicken. Roast, uncovered, for 25 minutes, or until the chicken is cooked through but moist.

4. To serve, squeeze the garlic out of the skin and spread on the chicken.

VARIATION: If you're looking to upgrade your roasted chicken, peel and mince the garlic. Using your fingers, carefully grasp the chicken skin and pull up gently, separating the skin from the meat. Then stuff the garlic between the skin and meat so it is spread out.

PER SERVING Calories: 229; Total Fat: 11g; Saturated Fat: 1g; Cholesterol: 84mg; Sodium: 27mg; Total Carbohydrates: 9g; Sugars: 2g; Protein: 27g

Roasted Lemon Chicken

9-BY-13-INCH ROASTING PAN

DAIRY-FREE · GLUTEN-FREE · NUT-FREE

The simplicity of this roasted lemon chicken makes it a surefire winner. Juicy chicken breasts are roasted under tart lemon slices, which add flavor and keep the meat tender. A handful of fresh baby kale and a quick dressing of olive oil, shallots, and red pepper flakes make it a meal.

SERVES 2
PREP TIME: 5 MINUTES
COOK TIME: 25 MINUTES

Nonstick cooking spray

4 boneless, skinless
chicken breasts

4 tablespoons extra-virgin
olive oil, divided

Salt

Freshly ground black pepper

2 lemons, sliced

¼ cup shallots, thinly sliced

1 teaspoon red pepper flakes

1 (5-ounce) package
baby kale

1. Preheat the oven to 450°F. Coat the roasting pan with non-stick cooking spray.

2. In the pan, rub the chicken with 2 tablespoons of olive oil and season generously with salt and pepper on both sides. Place the lemon slices on top of the chicken. Cover the pan (with aluminum foil if it doesn't have a cover) and roast for 15 minutes. Then uncover and roast for another 10 minutes, or until the chicken is cooked through but still moist.

3. In a small bowl, combine the shallots, red pepper flakes, and the remaining 2 tablespoons of olive oil, and season with salt and pepper.

4. Divide the kale evenly between two plates. Place the chicken on top, then drizzle with the dressing and serve.

VARIATION: Turn the leftovers into roasted lemon chicken spring rolls. Dip 1 rice wrapper in hot water for 2 seconds to soften. Lay on a flat surface on a kitchen towel, and add 2 spoonfuls of diced leftover chicken and kale in a line across the middle. Fold both sides inward, then tightly roll so the beginning meets the end.

PER SERVING Calories: 595; Total Fat: 32g; Saturated Fat: 4g; Cholesterol: 163mg; Sodium: 298mg; Total Carbohydrates: 11g; Sugars: 0g; Protein: 68g

Roasted Spicy Chicken Tortillas

9-BY-13-INCH ROASTING PAN

DAIRY-FREE · NUT-FREE

This restaurant-quality meal is perfect for a quick weeknight meal or a dinner party. Chicken breast is roasted with spicy poblano peppers and zucchini and then wrapped in warm tortillas. You can use either corn or flour tortillas, or offer a choice.

SERVES 4
PREP TIME: 10 MINUTES
COOK TIME: 25 MINUTES

Nonstick cooking spray

8 poblano peppers, seeded and halved

2 zucchini, sliced

2 tablespoons extra-virgin olive oil, divided

Salt

4 boneless, skinless chicken breasts

½ teaspoon dried oregano

Freshly ground black pepper

8 small corn or flour tortillas, warmed

1. Preheat the oven to 400°F. Coat the roasting pan with non-stick cooking spray.

2. In a large bowl, toss the poblano peppers and zucchini with 1 tablespoon of olive oil, and season with salt.

3. Season the chicken with the remaining 1 tablespoon of olive oil and the oregano, salt, and pepper and place in the roasting pan. Top the chicken with the poblano peppers and zucchini.

4. Cover with foil and roast for 15 minutes.

5. Uncover and roast for another 10 minutes, or until the chicken is cooked through. Enjoy served on the warm tortillas.

INGREDIENT TIP: Poblano peppers are one of the most useful and versatile chile peppers. They are mild, but they do have quite a bit more heat than a bell pepper. You can find them in the produce section.

PER SERVING Calories: 368; Total Fat: 11g; Saturated Fat: 1g; Cholesterol: 81mg; Sodium: 170mg; Total Carbohydrates: 33g; Sugars: 7g; Protein: 38g

Roasted Chicken with Thai Mango Salad

DAIRY-FREE · **GLUTEN-FREE** · **NUT-FREE**

Balancing the sweetness of mango, the acidity of lime juice, and sriracha's kick of heat makes this salad a winner. It also has a great interplay of textures—tender, juicy mango; crunchy nuts, if you like; peppers; lettuce; and meaty chicken.

SERVES 4
PREP TIME: 10 MINUTES
COOK TIME: 20 MINUTES

Nonstick cooking spray

4 boneless, skinless
chicken breasts

3 tablespoons extra-virgin
olive oil, divided

Salt

Freshly ground black pepper

1½ tablespoons sriracha

¼ cup freshly squeezed
lime juice

1 pound unripe mango,
peeled, pitted, and
thinly sliced

8 butter lettuce leaves, sliced

Optional garnish:

1 cup chopped fresh cilantro

2 tablespoons
chopped peanuts

1. Preheat the oven to 425°F. Coat the roasting pan with non-stick cooking spray.

2. Season the chicken with 1 tablespoon of olive oil and salt and pepper. Roast for 15 to 20 minutes, or until the chicken is cooked through but still moist. Let the chicken cool slightly, then slice it.

3. In a large bowl, whisk the sriracha, lime juice, and the remaining 2 tablespoons of oil, and season with salt and pepper. Add the mango, butter lettuce, and cooked chicken, and toss.

4. Sprinkle with the cilantro and peanuts, if using, and serve.

INGREDIENT TIP: Unripe mangoes are firmer and not nearly as sweet as the ripe ones. To pick one, press the mango gently and find something that feels very firm. If you don't plan to use it right away, keep the mango in the refrigerator to slow down the ripening process.

PER SERVING Calories: 320; Total Fat: 13g; Saturated Fat: 2g; Cholesterol: 81mg; Sodium: 272mg; Total Carbohydrates: 20g; Sugars: 15g; Protein: 34g

Roasted Pork Sandwiches

NUT-FREE

With succulent roasted pork, melty Swiss cheese, whole-grain mustard, and broccoli that's been caramelized in a hot oven, this sandwich is bound to quickly become a favorite. Even the pickiest of kids will be too busy enjoying the meaty, cheesy goodness to notice that they're eating healthy broccoli.

SERVES 4
PREP TIME: 5 MINUTES
COOK TIME: 20 MINUTES

Nonstick cooking spray

1 pound broccoli florets, cut into 2-inch pieces

2 tablespoons extra-virgin olive oil

Salt

Freshly ground black pepper

1 whole-wheat baguette, cut into 4 pieces

8 ounces deli roasted pork, sliced

4 Swiss cheese slices

1 tablespoon whole-grain mustard

1. Preheat the oven to 500°F, and place the rack 4 to 6 inches from the heat source. Coat the roasting pan with nonstick cooking spray.

2. In the pan, toss the broccoli with the olive oil, and season with salt and pepper. Roast for 20 minutes, or until tender.

3. Halve the baguette pieces lengthwise. Place a fourth of the pork and 1 slice of Swiss cheese on each baguette bottom. Broil for 2 minutes, or until the cheese is melted. Remove from the oven.

4. Add the broccoli florets on top of the cheese. Spread the mustard on the baguette tops, close up the sandwiches, and serve.

VARIATION: You can also use Dijon mustard on these sandwiches, or any hearty mustard that you love.

PER SERVING Calories: 515; Total Fat: 21g; Saturated Fat: 8g; Cholesterol: 86mg; Sodium: 1,826mg; Total Carbohydrates: 44g; Sugars: 4g; Protein: 41g

Rib Eye Steak Sandwiches

9-BY-13-INCH ROASTING PAN

DAIRY-FREE • NUT-FREE

There is almost nothing I love more than a rib eye steak sandwich on a warm summer's day, unless it's eating one in the garden surrounded by my family and friends. I make mine on toasted baguettes that have been brushed with garlic-infused olive oil. Yum!

SERVES 4
PREP TIME: 15 MINUTES
COOK TIME: 20 MINUTES

2 (1-pound) rib eye steaks, 1 inch thick

4 tablespoons extra-virgin olive oil, divided

Salt

Freshly ground black pepper

4 small baguettes

2 tablespoons fresh thyme

4 garlic cloves, finely chopped or mashed

2 cups arugula

1. Preheat the oven to 400°F.

2. Coat the steaks in 2 tablespoons of olive oil, and season generously with salt and pepper. Place in the pan and roast for 20 minutes, turning occasionally. Let them cool, then thinly slice the steaks.

3. While the steaks are roasting, cut open the baguettes and lightly toast them. In a small bowl, combine the remaining 2 tablespoons of olive oil with the thyme and garlic, and season with salt and pepper. Brush the insides of the baguettes with this mixture.

4. To serve, divide the steak slices among the baguettes and top with the arugula.

INGREDIENT TIP: When buying rib eye steak, look for white flecks in the meaty part (called marbling) so the steak will stay moist and hold its shape during cooking.

PER SERVING Calories: 757; Total Fat: 33g; Saturated Fat: 9g; Cholesterol: 100mg; Sodium: 759mg; Total Carbohydrates: 56g; Sugars: 3g; Protein: 57g

Pistachio-Crusted Lamb

10-BY-14-INCH ROASTING PAN

DAIRY-FREE

Did someone say lamb crusted in pistachios? Hello. This is the kind of dish I can't wait to sink my teeth into at the end of the day. It is a nutty, meaty meal that is both healthy and delicious—especially if you love a good lamb rack. Just add a glass of your favorite red wine and you are set.

SERVES 3 to 4
PREP TIME: 10 MINUTES
COOK TIME: 25 MINUTES,
PLUS 10 MINUTES TO REST

⅔ cup shelled pistachios

2 tablespoons breadcrumbs

Salt

Freshly ground black pepper

2 tablespoons Dijon mustard

2 (7-bone) racks of lamb, about 1½ pounds total

4 cups mixed salad greens, such as arugula, kale, and spinach

2 tablespoons extra-virgin olive oil

1. Preheat the oven to 400°F.

2. In a food processor, process the pistachios and breadcrumbs until you have fine crumbs. Season with salt and pepper.

3. Spread the mustard on the fatty side of each lamb rack and place in the roasting pan. Pat the pistachio mixture on top of the mustard. Roast for 20 to 25 minutes, or until the crust is golden and the lamb is pink in the center.

4. While the lamb is roasting, toss the mixed salad greens with the olive oil, and season with salt and pepper.

5. Remove the lamb from the oven and let rest for 10 minutes before cutting apart the ribs. Serve with the salad on the side.

INGREDIENT TIP: For faster prep, always buy shelled unsalted pistachios.

PER SERVING Calories: 582; Total Fat: 35g; Saturated Fat: 9g; Cholesterol: 150mg; Sodium: 295mg; Total Carbohydrates: 14g; Sugars: 2g; Protein: 52g

No-Cook Bowl

Mixing bowls may not seem very interesting, but I can safely say no kitchen can function properly without them. The recipes in this chapter require no cooking—just mixing in a bowl or assembling. Now for the real question: What kind of bowl do you need? Deep breath.

Strawberry-Spinach Salad, page 149

- **Stainless steel bowls** are the workhorse of mixing bowls—and they are cheap and durable. They are nonreactive, so they won't make even acidic food taste metallic.

- **Glass and ceramic bowls** are not bad either, but they are heavy. Glass is nonreactive, meaning it won't chemically affect the taste, color, or texture of your food. Plus it's microwaveable, and some tempered glass bowls are more durable and can be used in the oven or freezer. (Tempered glass is engineered using a heating and cooling process that makes it more durable and temperature resistant, as well as causing it to break into pebbles of glass rather than shards if broken.)

- **Plastic bowls** are inexpensive; however, some plastic can melt if it comes into contact with hot surfaces. Also, plastic can stain or absorb strong odors, like garlic. Always make sure the plastic bowls you use are free of BPA, BPS, phthalates, and PVC, as these chemicals can be harmful to your health.

- For most of the recipes in this chapter, you will need a 1.5-quart mixing bowl to prepare the dish. But if your space and budget permit, it's actually handy to have a **wide range of sizes and types** of bowls. The smallest bowl should hold 1 cup or less, which is perfect for beating a single egg or holding a portion of ingredients ready to be mixed into a recipe. Aside from that, an **assortment of five bowls** spanning a range of sizes from 2 cups to 5 quarts is perfect for most households and all the recipes in this book.

Prosciutto and Fig Jam Sandwiches

EXTRA-QUICK · DAIRY-FREE · NUT-FREE

The sweet-salty combo of prosciutto and fig jam makes an addictive sandwich filling. A handful of arugula adds a peppery bite. This simple sandwich is easy to whip up as a quick meal and ideal for brown-bagging lunch at work or taking on a picnic.

SERVES 4
PREP TIME: 5 MINUTES

4 teaspoons Dijon mustard

8 Italian bread slices, toasted

1 cup baby arugula

2 ounces prosciutto, very thinly sliced

2 tablespoons fig jam

1. Spread the mustard evenly over 4 bread slices. Top with the arugula and prosciutto.

2. Spread the fig jam on the remaining 4 bread slices and close up the sandwiches.

3. Cut each sandwich in half and serve.

VARIATION: For even more flavor, I like adding Brie or mascarpone cheese to these sandwiches; just note that they will no longer be dairy-free.

PER SERVING Calories: 198; Total Fat: 4g; Saturated Fat: 1g; Cholesterol: 23mg; Sodium: 805mg; Total Carbohydrates: 27g; Sugars: 6g; Protein: 13g

Chicken Satay Zoodles Bowl

BOWL

EXTRA-QUICK • DAIRY-FREE

This zoodle salad is full of hearty texture and creamy flavors. It takes shortcuts—like using shredded rotisserie chicken for the meat—without sacrificing the delicious flavor and texture combination. And the peanut sauce will keep for up to 1 week in an airtight container in the refrigerator.

SERVES 4
PREP TIME: 10 MINUTES

½ cup creamy peanut butter

1 tablespoon soy sauce

2 teaspoons honey

½ cup water, plus more
if needed

2 tablespoons extra-virgin
olive oil

1 (10-ounce) package
store-bought zucchini noodles
(about 8 cups), or make your
own from 2 large zucchini

2 cups shredded
rotisserie chicken

Optional garnish:

1 teaspoon red pepper flakes

1. In a blender, combine the peanut butter, soy sauce, honey, water, and olive oil. Process until smooth. Add more water if it is too thick.

2. In a large mixing bowl, combine the zoodles and chicken. Add the dressing and gently fold them together. Sprinkle on the red pepper flakes, if using, and serve.

PREP TIP: To shred a rotisserie chicken, first pull off the breasts and legs with your hands, or slide a knife along the breast bone to remove the breast meat. Remove the skin and bones, and use two forks to shred the meat.

PER SERVING Calories: 447; Total Fat: 29g; Saturated Fat: 6g; Cholesterol: 62mg; Sodium: 466mg; Total Carbohydrates: 40g; Sugars: 12g; Protein: 33g

Greek Pita Sandwiches

BOWL

EXTRA-QUICK · NUT-FREE

Pita bread is a simple, tasty vessel to hold any combination of fillings. This Greek pita sandwich is just what summer evenings call for with its fresh cucumber, sweet tomatoes, savory feta cheese, and tender chicken.

SERVES 4
PREP TIME: 5 MINUTES

2 cups diced cooked chicken

1 cup diced cucumber

1¼ cups halved cherry tomatoes

½ cup crumbled feta cheese

1 tablespoon extra-virgin olive oil

Salt

Freshly ground black pepper

4 (8-inch) whole-wheat pitas, halved

Optional garnish:

½ cup chopped fresh parsley

1. In a large bowl, combine the chicken, cucumber, tomatoes, feta, and olive oil, and season with salt and pepper. Mix well.

2. Spoon the mixture into the pita halves. Sprinkle the parsley on top, if using, and serve two halves to a plate.

INGREDIENT TIP: When possible, always try to get fresh feta cheese. You can place any leftover cheese in brine (a combination of 2 cups water and 1½ teaspoons salt) in an airtight container and refrigerate.

PER SERVING Calories: 369; Total Fat: 11g; Saturated Fat: 4g; Cholesterol: 71mg; Sodium: 636mg; Total Carbohydrates: 39g; Sugars: 3g; Protein: 30g

Turkey Wraps

EXTRA-QUICK · NUT-FREE

Make this wrap any time you want to eat healthy but are craving something indulgent. With avocado, Greek yogurt, and lean turkey breast, it's a delicious but guilt-free lunch. Wrap it up as an on-the-go lunch for work or school.

SERVES 4
PREP TIME: 5 MINUTES

2 tablespoons Greek yogurt

4 large flour tortillas

1 cup shredded lettuce leaves

8 ounces sliced cooked turkey breast

1 small avocado, peeled, pitted, and thinly sliced

1. Spread the Greek yogurt evenly on all the tortillas. Top with the lettuce, turkey breast, and avocado.

2. Roll up, cut in half, and serve.

VARIATION: To make this a bit healthier, use whole-grain or spinach tortillas.

PER SERVING Calories: 195; Total Fat: 8g; Saturated Fat: 1g; Cholesterol: 1mg; Sodium: 18mg; Total Carbohydrates: 16g; Sugars: 1g; Protein: 16g

TLT Sandwiches

EXTRA-QUICK · NUT-FREE

When you're in the mood for a tuna salad sandwich, but don't have time to make one, try this simple, deconstructed version. If you've got them, add a few pickle slices for flavor and texture.

SERVES 2
PREP TIME: 5 MINUTES

1 tablespoon light mayonnaise

4 whole-grain bread slices

4 butter lettuce leaves

1 beefsteak tomato, thinly sliced

1 (5-ounce) can water-packed light tuna, drained

Freshly ground black pepper

1. Spread the mayonnaise on all the bread slices. Top two slices of bread with the lettuce, tomato, and tuna.

2. Season generously with pepper, top each sandwich with a second slice of bread, and serve.

STORAGE TIP: Since mayonnaise is made from eggs, it must be refrigerated once it's been opened. Mayonnaise needs be tossed in the trash if its temperature reaches 50°F or higher for more than 8 hours.

PER SERVING Calories: 281; Total Fat: 5g; Saturated Fat: 1g; Cholesterol: 27mg; Sodium: 363mg; Total Carbohydrates: 30g; Sugars: 6g; Protein: 29g

Smoked Salmon Sliders

EXTRA-QUICK · NUT-FREE

The seductive combination of cream cheese and smoky salmon makes this sandwich a dreamy lunchtime option that is both simple and delicious. Add a sprinkle of "everything" bagel seasoning to replicate the flavors of bagels and lox.

SERVES 4
PREP TIME: 10 MINUTES

6 tablespoons light cream cheese

8 whole-grain slider buns

2 beefsteak tomatoes, each cut into 4 slices

8 lettuce leaves

8 ounces smoked salmon, thinly sliced

1. Spread the cream cheese on the bottom halves of all the buns. Top evenly with the tomato, lettuce, and smoked salmon, then the bun tops.

2. Serve the sliders two to a plate.

VARIATION: If you're looking for an alternative to cream cheese, try Greek yogurt and mix in 1½ teaspoons of chopped capers.

PER SERVING Calories: 278; Total Fat: 11g; Saturated Fat: 4g; Cholesterol: 24mg; Sodium: 1,241mg; Total Carbohydrates: 27g; Sugars: 5g; Protein: 18g

Smoked Salmon Rolls

BOWL

EXTRA-QUICK • NUT-FREE

I love using lavash—a thin, unleavened Middle Eastern flatbread—to make wraps, especially for a party. Spread a creamy mixture on the bread, then layer it with meat or fish and/or thinly sliced veggies, roll it up, and slice it for pretty pinwheels that can be eaten with fingers. This version combines smoked salmon with creamy Greek yogurt, wasabi (Japanese horseradish), juicy tomatoes, and peppery arugula.

SERVES 4
PREP TIME: 10 MINUTES

¼ cup Greek yogurt

1 teaspoon wasabi paste

2 lavash wraps

2 cucumbers, cut into 4-inch-long sticks

8 ounces smoked salmon, thinly sliced

Optional garnish:

2 cups baby arugula

2 tomatoes, halved and sliced

1. In a small bowl, combine the yogurt and wasabi paste. Spread the mixture on one side of each lavash wrap.

2. Add the cucumbers and smoked salmon. Top with the arugula and tomato, if using.

3. Roll up each wrap to the end, halve, and serve.

VARIATION: If you can't find wasabi paste, you can substitute horseradish.

PER SERVING Calories: 158; Total Fat: 3g; Saturated Fat: 1g; Cholesterol: 14mg; Sodium: 1,228mg; Total Carbohydrates: 17g; Sugars: 4g; Protein: 14g

Watermelon Caprese Salad

BOWL

EXTRA-QUICK · GLUTEN-FREE · NUT-FREE · VEGETARIAN

Sweet, juicy watermelon is a great match for salty and creamy mozzarella cheese. Fresh basil and a sweet, syrupy balsamic reduction heighten both flavors. This fresh salad is the perfect snack on a warm summer's evening, or pair it with a sandwich for a light meal. This recipe calls for mozzarella pearls—little balls of mozzarella—sold in the dairy case. They're often packed in liquid, so be sure to drain before using.

SERVES 4
PREP TIME: 10 MINUTES

1 small watermelon, cut into bite-size chunks (about 2 cups)

1 (8-ounce) package mozzarella pearls, drained

¼ cup chopped fresh basil

2 tablespoons extra-virgin olive oil

Salt

Freshly ground black pepper

2 tablespoons balsamic reduction

1. In a large bowl, combine the watermelon, mozzarella, and basil.

2. Toss with the olive oil, season with salt and pepper, then drizzle with the balsamic reduction and serve.

VARIATION: You can substitute regular balsamic vinegar if you cannot find balsamic reduction.

PER SERVING Calories: 253; Total Fat: 17g; Saturated Fat: 8g; Cholesterol: 50mg; Sodium: 220mg; Total Carbohydrates: 14g; Sugars: 11g; Protein: 11g

Strawberry-Spinach Salad

BOWL

EXTRA-QUICK · GLUTEN-FREE · VEGETARIAN

Bright red, juicy, sweet summer strawberries are the star of this salad, but tender spinach leaves, tangy balsamic vinegar, crunchy slivered almonds, and salty blue cheese all play essential supporting roles. Serve this as a simple and light lunch or alongside grilled meats.

SERVES 2
PREP TIME: 10 MINUTES

1 tablespoon
balsamic vinegar

½ cup extra-virgin olive oil

Salt

Freshly ground black pepper

1 (10-ounce) package fresh
baby spinach, washed, dried,
and torn into pieces

2 cups sliced strawberries

¼ cup blanched
slivered almonds

½ cup crumbled blue cheese

1. In a small bowl, mix the balsamic vinegar and olive oil, and season with salt and pepper.

2. In a large bowl, pour the balsamic dressing over the spinach. Add the strawberries and almonds, and gently toss to coat.

3. Sprinkle with the blue cheese before serving.

VARIATION: You could use roughly chopped walnuts or pecans instead of (or in addition to) the almonds.

PER SERVING Calories: 706; Total Fat: 67g; Saturated Fat: 13g; Cholesterol: 25mg; Sodium: 664mg; Total Carbohydrates: 21g; Sugars: 10g; Protein: 15g

 # Kale Salad

BOWL

EXTRA-QUICK · GLUTEN-FREE · NUT-FREE · VEGETARIAN

Kale made a meteoric rise up the popularity charts a few years ago, and the love for it doesn't seem to be waning. This simple, delicious salad shows you exactly why it is so well loved. Lemon, garlic, and Parmesan cheese complement the slightly bitter greens well.

SERVES 4
PREP TIME: 10 MINUTES

4 cups finely chopped lacinato kale

½ small red onion, thinly sliced

1 garlic clove, finely chopped

2 tablespoons grated Parmesan cheese

Juice of 1 lemon

¼ cup extra-virgin olive oil

Salt

Freshly ground black pepper

Optional garnish:

1 tablespoon roasted pumpkin seeds (pepitas)

½ cup pomegranate seeds

1. In a large bowl, combine the kale and red onion.

2. In a small bowl, mix together the garlic, Parmesan cheese, lemon juice, and olive oil. Season with salt and pepper.

3. Pour the dressing over the salad, and use your fingers to rub the dressing into the kale leaves. Squeeze them with moderate pressure, then squeeze again to break down the fibers in the kale, making it a lot more tender and easier to chew. Let the salad sit for at least 5 minutes, and up to a day.

4. Just before serving, sprinkle the pumpkin and pomegranate seeds on top, if using.

INGREDIENT TIP: Lacinto kale is also sometimes called Tuscan or dinosaur kale. It's got flat, very-dark-green leaves and is a bit milder in taste than curly kale. To prepare it, discard the stems and center ribs.

PER SERVING Calories: 157; Total Fat: 13g; Saturated Fat: 2g; Cholesterol: 3mg; Sodium: 101mg; Total Carbohydrates: 8g; Sugars: 0g; Protein: 3g

Caprese Zoodles

BOWL

EXTRA-QUICK · GLUTEN-FREE · NUT-FREE · VEGETARIAN

Zoodles—spiralized zucchini—make a great low-carb, gluten-free pasta alternative. Tossing the zoodles with salt and olive oil and letting them rest for 15 minutes is the trick to making them tender and tasty. Add ripe cherry tomatoes, pearls of mozzarella cheese, fresh basil, and a sweet-tart balsamic reduction for a quick and satisfying "pasta" salad.

SERVES 4
PREP TIME: 5 MINUTES,
PLUS 15 MINUTES TO REST

1 (10-ounce) package store-bought zucchini noodles (about 8 cups), or make your own from 2 large zucchini

2 tablespoons extra-virgin olive oil

Salt

Freshly ground black pepper

2 cups cherry tomatoes, halved

1 (8-ounce) package mozzarella pearls, drained

¼ cup chopped fresh basil

2 tablespoons balsamic reduction

1. In a large bowl, combine the zoodles with the olive oil, and season with salt and pepper. Let rest for 15 minutes.

2. Add the tomatoes, mozzarella, and basil, and toss gently. Drizzle with the balsamic reduction and serve.

PREP TIP: You can make your own zoodles using a mandoline. Halve the zucchini lengthwise with a knife, then slice it on a mandoline. When all zucchini are sliced, simply cut them lengthwise to create thin zoodles.

PER SERVING Calories: 298; Total Fat: 18g; Saturated Fat: 8g; Cholesterol: 50mg; Sodium: 256mg; Total Carbohydrates: 22g; Sugars: 15g; Protein: 15g

Fresh Spring Roll Bowl

BOWL

EXTRA-QUICK · DAIRY-FREE · VEGAN

This quick noodle bowl delivers all the fresh flavors of fresh spring rolls, but without the tedious filling and rolling. Thin rice noodles don't even need to be cooked. A few minutes of soaking in hot water turns them tender, and they're a perfect backdrop for crisp veggies and rich, nutty peanut sauce. If you don't have chunky peanut butter, you can use creamy, but it will give you a less crunchy texture. Almond or cashew butter will also work.

SERVES 4
PREP TIME: 10 MINUTES

1 (8-ounce) package thin rice noodles (rice vermicelli)

1 cup chunky peanut butter

⅓ cup soy sauce

2 cups hot water, as needed

2 cups shredded carrots

2 English cucumbers, sliced

Optional garnish:

Chopped peanuts

Chopped fresh cilantro

1. To prepare the noodles, soak them in a large bowl of hot water for 10 to 15 minutes (depending on the thickness), or until they're pliable. Drain the noodles and rinse under cold water to stop the cooking, then return to the bowl.

2. To make the sauce, in a medium bowl, combine the peanut butter and soy sauce. Mix well. Thin the sauce by slowly adding hot water (you probably won't use it all) until you reach the desired consistency. It should be smooth but not too watery.

3. Add the carrots and cucumbers to the bowl with the drained rice noodles and toss. Mix in the sauce. Garnish with the chopped peanuts and cilantro, if using, and serve.

INGREDIENT TIP: Rice noodles are made out of rice flour and water, or rice that is soaked, ground into paste, rolled, and cut into noodles. Rice noodles are much more delicate and fragile compared to other noodles, and they don't need to be boiled. They are also gluten-free. You can find rice noodles in the international aisle in the grocery store. You can also substitute whole-wheat angel-hair pasta or vermicelli if your store does not carry rice noodles.

PER SERVING Calories: 649; Total Fat: 33g; Saturated Fat: 5g; Cholesterol: 0mg; Sodium: 1,552mg; Total Carbohydrates: 72g; Sugars: 11g; Protein: 22g

Elegant Tuna Salad

BOWL

EXTRA-QUICK · DAIRY-FREE · GLUTEN-FREE · NUT-FREE

This salad is so simple, but its flavors will transport you to the South of France. Use ripe summer tomatoes and a good-quality canned tuna to really do this salad justice. It makes the perfect poolside lunch or light dinner on a warm evening. For a heartier salad, add halved hard-boiled eggs and a handful of black olives.

SERVES 4
PREP TIME: 10 MINUTES

2 teaspoons Dijon mustard

6 tablespoons extra-virgin olive oil

Juice of 1 lemon

Salt

Freshly ground black pepper

1 large romaine lettuce head, torn into bite-size pieces

2 (5-ounce) cans water-packed light tuna, drained

2 large vine-ripened tomatoes, cut into wedges

1. To make the dressing, in a medium bowl, whisk together the mustard and oil. Add the lemon juice, and season with salt and pepper.

2. In a large serving bowl, gently toss together the lettuce, tuna, and tomato wedges. Add the dressing, toss again to coat, and serve.

PREP TIP: The salad dressing can be made ahead of time and refrigerated for up to 1 week in a jar with a lid.

PER SERVING Calories: 320; Total Fat: 22g; Saturated Fat: 3g; Cholesterol: 25mg; Sodium: 124mg; Total Carbohydrates: 9g; Sugars: 4g; Protein: 24g

Chicken-Edamame Salad

BOWL

EXTRA-QUICK · DAIRY-FREE · GLUTEN-FREE · NUT-FREE

Sure, it's "just" a salad, but this no-cook bowl is so full of goodies that it truly satisfies like a meal. With edamame (soy beans), chicken, and black beans, it's loaded with protein. Corn kernels and sweet red bell pepper add color and texture.

SERVES 2
PREP TIME: 5 MINUTES

2 cups cooked,
shelled edamame

2 cups diced cooked chicken

2 cups frozen or roasted corn,
thawed if frozen

1 red bell pepper, seeded
and diced

1 (14-ounce) can black beans,
rinsed and drained

2 tablespoons extra-virgin
olive oil

Salt

Freshly ground black pepper

Optional garnish:

1 tablespoon thinly sliced
fresh basil

1. In a large bowl, combine the edamame, chicken, corn, bell pepper, black beans, and olive oil. Toss gently, then season with salt and pepper.

2. Scatter the basil on top, if using, and serve.

INGREDIENT TIP: To roast corn kernels on a stove top, heat 1 tablespoon of extra-virgin olive oil in a 10-inch skillet over medium-high heat. Add the corn and cook for 10 to 12 minutes, or until the corn starts to brown.

PER SERVING Calories: 829; Total Fat: 26g; Saturated Fat: 4g; Cholesterol: 108mg; Sodium: 202mg; Total Carbohydrates: 83g; Sugars: 10g; Protein: 72g

Thai Peanut-Chicken Salad

BOWL

EXTRA-QUICK · DAIRY-FREE

Supermarket rotisserie chicken is a great ingredient for quick dinners. You can eat it hot straight from the store, shred it and use it as a filling for sandwiches or wraps, toss it with cooked pasta and sauce, or use it to turn a salad into a meal. A creamy peanut-lime dressing gives this salad delicious Thai flavor.

SERVES 4
PREP TIME: 10 MINUTES

½ cup creamy peanut butter

1 tablespoon reduced-sodium soy sauce

1 tablespoon freshly squeezed lime juice

2 cups shredded rotisserie chicken

1 (5-ounce) package mixed salad greens, such as arugula, kale, and spinach

Optional garnish:

1 cup fresh cilantro

2 tablespoons chopped unsalted roasted peanuts

1. To make the dressing, in a medium bowl, combine the peanut butter, soy sauce, and lime juice.

2. In a large bowl, combine the chicken and mixed salad greens. Pour on the dressing, and toss to coat. Top with the cilantro and roasted peanuts, if using, and serve.

VARIATION: Other nut butters and seed butters, such as almond, sunflower, or cashew, would work just as well in this recipe.

PER SERVING Calories: 323; Total Fat: 18g; Saturated Fat: 4g; Cholesterol: 54mg; Sodium: 440mg; Total Carbohydrates: 12g; Sugars: 3g; Protein: 30g

The Dirty Dozen™ and the Clean Fifteen™

A nonprofit environmental watchdog organization called Environmental Working Group (EWG) looks at data supplied by the U.S. Department of Agriculture (USDA) and the Food and Drug Administration (FDA) about pesticide residues. Each year it compiles a list of the best and worst pesticide loads found in commercial crops. You can use these lists to decide which fruits and vegetables to buy organic to minimize your exposure to pesticides and which produce is considered safe enough to buy conventionally. This does not mean they are pesticide-free, though, so wash these fruits and vegetables thoroughly.

THE DIRTY DOZEN™		THE CLEAN FIFTEEN™	
The 2018 Dirty Dozen™ includes the following produce. These are considered among the year's most important produce to buy organic:		The least critical to buy organically are the Clean Fifteen™ list. The following are on the 2018 list:	
apples	spinach	asparagus	kiwis
celery	strawberries	avocados	mangoes
cherries	sweet bell peppers	broccoli	onions
grapes	tomatoes	cabbages	papayas
nectarines		cantaloupes	pineapples
peaches	*Additionally, nearly three-quarters of hot pepper samples contained pesticide residues	cauliflower	sweet corn
pears		eggplants	sweet peas (frozen)
potatoes		honeydew melons	

Measurement Conversions

Volume Equivalents (Liquid)

STANDARD	U.S. STANDARD (OUNCES)	METRIC (APPROXIMATE)
2 tablespoons	1 fl. oz.	30 mL
¼ cup	2 fl. oz.	60 mL
½ cup	4 fl. oz.	120 mL
1 cup	8 fl. oz.	240 mL
1½ cups	12 fl. oz.	355 mL
2 cups or 1 pint	16 fl. oz.	475 mL
4 cups or 1 quart	32 fl. oz.	1 L
1 gallon	128 fl. oz.	4 L

Oven Temperatures

FAHRENHEIT (F)	CELSIUS (C) (APPROXIMATE)
250°	120°
300°	150°
325°	165°
350°	180°
375°	190°
400°	200°
425°	220°
450°	230°

Volume Equivalents (Dry)

STANDARD	METRIC (APPROXIMATE)
⅛ teaspoon	0.5 mL
¼ teaspoon	1 mL
½ teaspoon	2 mL
¾ teaspoon	4 mL
1 teaspoon	5 mL
1 tablespoon	15 mL
¼ cup	59 mL
⅓ cup	79 mL
½ cup	118 mL
⅔ cup	156 mL
¾ cup	177 mL
1 cup	235 mL
2 cups or 1 pint	475 mL
3 cups	700 mL
4 cups or 1 quart	1 L

Weight Equivalents

STANDARD	METRIC (APPROXIMATE)
½ ounce	15 g
1 ounce	30 g
2 ounces	60 g
4 ounces	115 g
8 ounces	225 g
12 ounces	340 g
16 ounces or 1 pound	455 g

Recipe Index

Index

Acknowledgments

Working on this cookbook and seeing it come to fruition has been an incredible experience, and one that could not have been done without the support of those around me.

The first—and biggest—thank you goes to my husband, my number one taste tester who has supported me through all of my ventures and has kept me (mostly) sane throughout the journey.

To Gideon and Lindy, I wouldn't be writing this today if it wasn't for you.

To all my family and friends, thank you for trying my delicious (and not so delicious) dishes and for giving such valuable feedback. You guys are amazing!

To my editor, Vanessa Ta, and the rest of the Callisto Media team, thank you for this opportunity and for making my dream become an amazing reality.

And most importantly, to my readers, without you, none of this would be possible, so from the bottom of my heart, THANK YOU.

About the Author

LINDA KURNIADI grew up in Indonesia before moving to San Francisco for her studies. Living so far from home, missing the flavors of her mom's cooking, and surviving on a student's budget, Linda was inspired to try out her own recipes and share them on her blog, *Simply Healthyish Recipes*.

To her delight, Linda could create delicious dishes that were zesty, healthy, and comforting. One recipe led to another, and before she knew it, she had enough recipes to create a book.

Her recipes have been featured on *Better Homes and Gardens*, MSN.com, *Country Living Magazine*, *Taste of Home Magazine*, the Feed Feed, and many more. For more recipes, visit SimplyHealthyish.com.